REFUGEES

Clarissa Aykroyd

THE CHANGING
Face of North America:
IMMIGRATION SINCE 1965

Asylees

Chinese Immigration

Cuban Immigration

Deported Aliens

Filipino Immigration

Haitian Immigration

Immigration from Central America

Immigration from the Dominican Republic

Immigration from the Former Yugoslavia

Immigration from the Middle East

Immigration from South America

Indian Immigration

Korean Immigration

Mexican Immigration

Refugees

Vietnamese Immigration

REFUGEES

Clarissa Aykroyd

MASON CREST PUBLISHERS
PHILADELPHIA

Produced by OTTN Publishing, Stockton, New Jersey

Mason Crest Publishers
370 Reed Road
Broomall, PA 19008
www.masoncrest.com

First printing

1 3 5 7 9 8 6 4 2

Library of Congress Cataloging-in-Publication Data

Aykroyd, Clarissa.
  Refugees / Clarissa Aykroyd.
      p. cm. — (The changing face of North America)
Summary: A history of refugees to the United States and Canada, particularly during the
twentieth century, and an overview of the process refugees undergo when they arrive in North America.
Includes bibliographical references and index.
  ISBN 1-59084-692-3
1. Refugees—North America. 2. North America—Emigration and immigration.
[1. Refugees. 2. Refugees—Canada. 3. United States—Emigration and immigration—History—20th century.
4. Canada—Emigration and immigration—History—20th century.] I. Title. II. Series.
  HV640.4.N6A95 2004
  305.9'06914'0973—dc22
                              2003013291

THE CHANGING
Face of North America:
IMMIGRATION SINCE 1965

CONTENTS

Introduction
Senator Edward M. Kennedy   6

Foreword
Marian L. Smith   8
Peter A. Hammerschmidt   11

The Refugee in the 20th Century   15

Refugee Policy Through the Years 27

The Boat People   51

Crisis in the Caribbean   61

Refugees from the Middle East   77

Refugees from Europe   87

The Challenges Ahead   99

Famous Refugees   102

Glossary   103

Further Reading   104

Internet Resources   105

Index   106

INTRODUCTION

THE CHANGING FACE OF AMERICA

By Senator Edward M. Kennedy

America is proud of its heritage and history as a nation of immigrants, and my own family is an example. All eight of my great-grandparents were immigrants who left Ireland a century and a half ago, when that land was devastated by the massive famine caused by the potato blight. When I was a young boy, my grandfather used to take me down to the docks in Boston and regale me with stories about the Great Famine and the waves of Irish immigrants who came to America seeking a better life. He talked of how the Irish left their marks in Boston and across the nation, enduring many hardships and harsh discrimination, but also building the railroads, digging the canals, settling the West, and filling the factories of a growing America. According to one well-known saying of the time, "under every railroad tie, an Irishman is buried."

America was the promised land for them, as it has been for so many other immigrants who have found shelter, hope, opportunity, and freedom. Immigrants have always been an indispensable part of our nation. They have contributed immensely to our communities, created new jobs and whole new industries, served in our armed forces, and helped make America the continuing land of promise that it is today.

The inspiring poem by Emma Lazarus, inscribed on the pedestal of the Statue of Liberty in New York Harbor, is America's welcome to all immigrants:

Give me your tired, your poor,
Your huddled masses yearning to breathe free,
The wretched refuse of your teeming shore,
Send these, the homeless, tempest-tossed, to me:
I lift my lamp beside the golden door.

The period since September 11, 2001, has been particularly challenging for immigrants. Since the horrifying terrorist attacks, there has been a resurgence of anti-immigrant attitudes and behavior. We all agree that our borders must be safe and secure. Yet, at the same time, we must safeguard the entry of the millions of persons who come to the United States legally each year as immigrants, visitors, scholars, students, and workers. The "golden door" must stay open. We must recognize that immigration is not the problem—terrorism is. We must identify and isolate the terrorists, and not isolate America.

One of my most important responsibilities in the Senate is the preservation of basic rights and basic fairness in the application of our immigration laws, so that new generations of immigrants in our own time and for all time will have the same opportunity that my great-grandparents had when they arrived in America.

Immigration is beneficial for the United States and for countries throughout the world. It is no coincidence that two hundred years ago, our nations' founders chose *E Pluribus Unum*—"out of many, one"—as America's motto. These words, chosen by Benjamin Franklin, John Adams, and Thomas Jefferson, refer to the ideal that separate colonies can be transformed into one united nation. Today, this ideal has come to apply to individuals as well. Our diversity is our strength. We are a nation of immigrants, and we always will be.

Foreword

The Changing Face of the United States

Marian L. Smith, historian
U.S. Immigration and Naturalization Service

Americans commonly assume that immigration today is very different than immigration of the past. The immigrants themselves appear to be unlike immigrants of earlier eras. Their language, their dress, their food, and their ways seem strange. At times people fear too many of these new immigrants will destroy the America they know. But has anything really changed? Do new immigrants have any different effect on America than old immigrants a century ago? Is the American fear of too much immigration a new development? Do immigrants really change America more than America changes the immigrants? The very subject of immigration raises many questions.

In the United States, immigration is more than a chapter in a history book. It is a continuous thread that links the present moment to the first settlers on North American shores. From the first colonists' arrival until today, immigrants have been met by Americans who both welcomed and feared them. Immigrant contributions were always welcome—on the farm, in the fields, and in the factories. Welcoming the poor, the persecuted, and the "huddled masses" became an American principle. Beginning with the original Pilgrims' flight from religious persecution in the 1600s, through the Irish migration to escape starvation in the 1800s, to the relocation of Central Americans seeking refuge from civil wars in the 1980s and 1990s, the United States has considered itself a haven for the destitute and the oppressed.

But there was also concern that immigrants would not adopt American ways, habits, or language. Too many immigrants might overwhelm America. If so, the dream of the Founding Fathers for United States government and society would be destroyed. For this reason, throughout American history some have argued that limiting or ending immigration is our patriotic duty. Benjamin Franklin feared there were so many German immigrants in Pennsylvania the Colonial Legislature would begin speaking German. "Progressive" leaders of the early 1900s feared that immigrants who could not read and understand the English language were not only exploited by "big business," but also served as the foundation for "machine politics" that undermined the U.S. Constitution. This theme continues today, usually voiced by those who bear no malice toward immigrants but who want to preserve American ideals.

Have immigrants changed? In colonial days, when most colonists were of English descent, they considered Germans, Swiss, and French immigrants as different. They were not "one of us" because they spoke a different language. Generations later, Americans of German or French descent viewed Polish, Italian, and Russian immigrants as strange. They were not "like us" because they had a different religion, or because they did not come from a tradition of constitutional government. Recently, Americans of Polish or Italian descent have seen Nicaraguan, Pakistani, or Vietnamese immigrants as too different to be included. It has long been said of American immigration that the latest ones to arrive usually want to close the door behind them.

It is important to remember that fear of individual immigrant groups seldom lasted, and always lessened. Benjamin Franklin's anxiety over German immigrants disappeared after those immigrants' sons and daughters helped the nation gain independence in the Revolutionary War. The Irish of the mid-1800s were among the most hated immigrants, but today we all wear green on St. Patrick's Day. While a century ago it was feared that Italian and other Catholic immigrants would vote as directed by the Pope, today that controversy is only a vague memory. Unfortunately, some ethnic groups continue their efforts to earn acceptance. The African

Americans' struggle continues, and some Asian Americans, whose families have been in America for generations, are the victims of current anti-immigrant sentiment.

Time changes both immigrants and America. Each wave of new immigrants, with their strange language and habits, eventually grows old and passes away. Their American-born children speak English. The immigrants' grandchildren are completely American. The strange foods of their ancestors—spaghetti, baklava, hummus, or tofu—become common in any American restaurant or grocery store. Much of what the immigrants brought to these shores is lost, principally their language. And what is gained becomes as American as St. Patrick's Day, Hanukkah, or Cinco de Mayo, and we forget that it was once something foreign.

Recent immigrants are all around us. They come from every corner of the earth to join in the American Dream. They will continue to help make the American Dream a reality, just as all the immigrants who came before them have done.

FOREWORD

THE CHANGING FACE OF CANADA

Peter A. Hammerschmidt
First Secretary, Permanent Mission of Canada to the United Nations

Throughout Canada's history, immigration has shaped and defined the very character of Canadian society. The migration of peoples from every part of the world into Canada has profoundly changed the way we look, speak, eat, and live. Through close and distant relatives who left their lands in search of a better life, all Canadians have links to immigrant pasts. We are a nation built by and of immigrants.

Two parallel forces have shaped the history of Canadian immigration. The enormous diversity of Canada's immigrant population is the most obvious. In the beginning came the enterprising settlers of the "New World," the French and English colonists. Soon after came the Scottish, Irish, and Northern and Central European farmers of the 1700s and 1800s. As the country expanded westward during the mid-1800s, migrant workers began arriving from China, Japan, and other Asian countries. And the turbulent twentieth century brought an even greater variety of immigrants to Canada, from the Caribbean, Africa, India, and Southeast Asia.

So while English- and French-Canadians are the largest ethnic groups in the country today, neither group alone represents a majority of the population. A large and vibrant multicultural mix makes up the rest, particularly in Canada's major cities. Toronto, Vancouver, and Montreal alone are home to people from over 200 ethnic groups!

Less obvious but equally important in the evolution of Canadian immigration has been hope. The promise of a better life lured Europeans and Americans seeking cheap (sometimes even free) farmland. Thousands of Scots and Irish arrived to escape grinding poverty and starvation. Others came for freedom, to escape religious and political persecution. Canada has long been a haven to the world's dispossessed and disenfranchised—Dutch and German farmers cast out for their religious beliefs, black slaves fleeing the United States, and political refugees of despotic regimes in Europe, Africa, Asia, and South America.

The two forces of diversity and hope, so central to Canada's past, also shaped the modern era of Canadian immigration. Following the Second World War, Canada drew heavily on these influences to forge trailblazing immigration initiatives.

The catalyst for change was the adoption of the Canadian Bill of Rights in 1960. Recognizing its growing diversity and Canadians' changing attitudes towards racism, the government passed a federal statute barring discrimination on the grounds of race, national origin, color, religion, or sex. Effectively rejecting the discriminatory elements in Canadian immigration policy, the Bill of Rights forced the introduction of a new policy in 1962. The focus of immigration abruptly switched from national origin to the individual's potential contribution to Canadian society. The door to Canada was now open to every corner of the world.

Welcoming those seeking new hopes in a new land has also been a feature of Canadian immigration in the modern era. The focus on economic immigration has increased along with Canada's steadily growing economy, but political immigration has also been encouraged. Since 1945, Canada has admitted tens of thousands of displaced persons, including Jewish Holocaust survivors, victims of Soviet crackdowns in Hungary and Czechoslovakia, and refugees from political upheaval in Uganda, Chile, and Vietnam.

Prior to 1978, however, these political refugees were admitted as an exception to normal immigration procedures. That year, Canada revamped its refugee policy with a new Immigration Act that explicit-ly affirmed Canada's commitment to the resettlement of refugees from oppression. Today, the admission of refugees remains a central part of Canadian immigration law and regulations.

Amendments to economic and political immigration policy continued during the 1980s and 1990s, refining further the bold steps taken during the modern era. Together, these initiatives have turned Canada into one of the world's few truly multicultural states.

Unlike the process of assimilation into a "melting pot" of cultures, immigrants to Canada are more likely to retain their cultural identity, beliefs, and practices. This is the source of some of Canada's greatest strengths as a society. And as a truly multicultural nation, diversity is not seen as a threat to Canadian identity. Quite the contrary—diversity *is* Canadian identity.

1 THE REFUGEE IN THE 20TH CENTURY

The following account was presented by Monica Tito Ayuen to the U.S. Committee for Refugees. Monica is from southern Sudan, a region that has been ravaged by continuous civil war for nearly two decades.

I completed eight years of primary school and four years of secondary education in my home area. I earned a scholarship to study at a university in Egypt, but I could not leave Sudan because of the war. Those school days now seem long ago.

The attack that pushed my husband, my two young children, and me from home occurred in March 1992. We were chased away by government troops. We were shot at all day. I was temporarily separated from my husband and children in the mayhem. My father was killed, and so were my uncles. There was little time to take anything. We just ran.

The first night, I was in a forest. I slept in a tree because I was afraid of the wild animals. We ate leaves of plants and wild fruits along the way. As we fled on foot for two months, my family and I tried to travel in the evening when temperatures were a bit cooler. I eventually reached the safety of a camp for displaced persons in extreme southern Sudan, near the border with Uganda. For my family and me, life soon settled into a bearable routine despite the hardships of being uprooted.

But the tranquility did not last. Less than two years later, government troops attacked the camp where I lived and worked. With a four-year-old son and a two-year-old daughter in tow, I found that escape was difficult. The enemy followed me and shot at me. I saw dead bodies while running. I carried our two kids, one by hand, and one on my back. We prayed to God to save our lives. . . .

◀ Young Sudanese refugees look after their younger siblings in a refugee camp in Bonga, Ethiopia, 2003. Since the late 1990s, the United States and Canada have accepted refugees fleeing civil war in Sudan.

I ran 40 miles with my family, to a new camp where I have lived for the past four years. This place is not good, even the flies bite here. I want to go back home, but I cannot safely return home. Life as an uprooted person has again settled back into a routine for me, but this time with fewer blankets, fewer clothes, and a shortage of medicines.

While some of the details of Monica's story differ from those of other refugees, for people who follow refugee crises, her story is far too familiar.

Sudan is Africa's largest country. Located to the south of Egypt, in northeastern Africa, this vast land covers nearly a million square miles (2,589,990 square kilometers), and boasts a wide variety of landscapes: sprawling deserts, dense rain-forests, and the valley of the Nile River. It is also a country of great ethnic diversity, with a population comprised of Arabs, Fur, Dinka, Beja, Nuba, and other groups.

Since the 1950s, a series of civil wars have torn Sudan apart. These wars have started because of ethnic and religious differences, political crises, famine, and poverty. More than a million people have died. Others have had to flee from one place to another within Sudan, or have had to leave the country altogether—to become refugees.

Many of the refugee victims of Sudan's civil wars have been children. In the 1980s, thousands of these children became known as the "Lost Boys." The armies of the civil wars forced some of them to become soldiers. Others spent years in refugee camps. For many of the Lost Boys, hope finally came from a place far away from their original homes. In the late 1990s, the

Fridtjof Nansen

The first High Commissioner for Refugees appointed by the League of Nations, Fridtjof Nansen, was a former Arctic explorer. He completed the first ever crossing of Greenland, which he achieved on skis with five other traveling companions. The first travel documents issued by the High Commissioner were known as "Nansen passports." For his service to refugees, Nansen received the Nobel Peace Prize in 1922.

United States and Canada made a special effort to give new homes in North America to these young refugees. The United States agreed to take up to 3,600 of the children.

This resettlement program allowed the children to start again in different areas of North America. They went to places as far apart as Richmond, Virginia, and Vancouver, British Columbia, on the west coast of Canada. Now, they faced a new set of challenges, including unfamiliar technology and culture shock. Even the weather was completely different. None of the children had ever seen snow before they came to North America. For a refugee, the move to a new country is only the beginning.

The official definition of *refugee* has changed over many decades, but the present version shared by the Canadian and U.S. governments states that a refugee is someone who is outside his or her home country and who cannot return because of the threat of violence or persecution. According to the law, to qualify as a refugee, this persecution must be "on account of race, religion, nationality, membership in a particular social group, or political opinion." In Canada, those who fall under the most common refugee category, the "Convention Refugees Abroad Class," must have one or more of the same reasons to fear persecution.

History of the Refugee

There have always been situations that create refugees. Throughout history, wars, persecution, and other crises have forced people to flee to other countries. The wars of the early 20th century produced millions of refugees, persuading governments and international organizations to begin to look for new ways to help displaced people. Since the end of World War I (1914–18), many of the world's most powerful politicians and organizations have struggled to decide what makes a person a refugee, and how to help these people. Often, their decisions have created new and better ways to help refugees. Sometimes, however, these decisions have made things more difficult for people forced to leave their countries because of desperate situations.

Before the 20th century, many governments welcomed refugees from other countries. They saw these people as a means of improving their economies, or as new additions to the workforce and the army, so refugees did not face many restrictions. In the early years of the 20th century, however, many groups of people began to change their attitude toward refugees. Governments began to view the unrestricted movement of refugees as a threat to their stability or, mistakenly, to the employment prospects for natives. Before World War I, large empires had existed in Europe; at the end of the war, these empires split up into smaller nation-states. Many of the new nations refused to accept certain people as citizens if they came from the "wrong" ethnic background, and so these people became refugees.

The plight of the refugees from Russia in the 1920s indicated to the world the need for action. Between 1917 and 1923, Russia experienced a revolution, a civil war, and a major famine. The Soviet Union, formed in 1922, denied citizenship to many of the refugees created by these events. International

Displaced Russians advance eastward, fleeing the German invasion of 1941. With the uprooting of hundreds of thousands of refugees during World War II, many world leaders were convinced of the need to establish an international refugee organization.

Internally Displaced Persons

The term *refugee* does not include the large number of internally displaced persons (IDPs), who have had to leave their homes but who have remained within their own country. During the 1990s alone, there were between 7 and 8 million IDPs worldwide, according to the World Refugee Survey 2000. Displaced people may have to flee their homes or countries because of natural disasters such as floods or earthquakes. Most people agree that victims of such disasters are not refugees in the legal sense of the word.

organizations such as the Red Cross did not have enough resources to help the vast numbers of Russian refugees. In 1921, a newly formed organization for international security called the League of Nations established the Office of the High Commissioner for Refugees. The person who took this position was expected to give assistance to the Russian refugees and, if possible, to help repatriate them (send them back to their original country).

Leading up to the Geneva Convention

The first appointed High Commissioner for Refugees was Fridtjof Nansen, who remained in office until his death in 1930. Nansen immediately began looking for ways to help refugees, especially those in Eastern Europe. During the 1920s, he provided travel documents to not only Russians but also Armenian, Assyrian, and Turkish refugees. The documents made it easier for refugees to move legally from one place to another. Following the 1933 League of Nations Convention Relating to the International Status of Refugees, which guaranteed basic rights to refugees, displaced people now had a better chance to remain in the countries to which they had fled. Most refugees wanted to return to their original country—and most countries preferred to send them home—though this was often not a viable option.

During the 1930s, refugees fled the Nazi regime in Germany

and Austria. Others fled from the totalitarian states in Italy and Spain. Many countries were not happy to receive these refugees, pushing governments to reduce the number of refugees accepted as immigrants. Some countries did not want to accept anyone who did not belong to a certain ethnic group; for instance, the United States and Canada preferred to take people who were British or Irish.

During World War II (1939–45), the refugee problem worsened dramatically and many Jews in Europe could not escape persecution and, later, death, due to immigration restrictions around the world, including those in Canada and the United States. After World War II, to address the crisis of the many Europeans made homeless by the war, the United States developed the International Refugee Organization (IRO) in 1946. The IRO was an agency of the United Nations (UN), which

After being released from the Buchenwald concentration camp in Germany, 1945, Jewish refugee children depart for Palestine, where many European Jewish refugees resettled after World War II ended. Many other victims of the Nazi regime relocated to the United States and Canada.

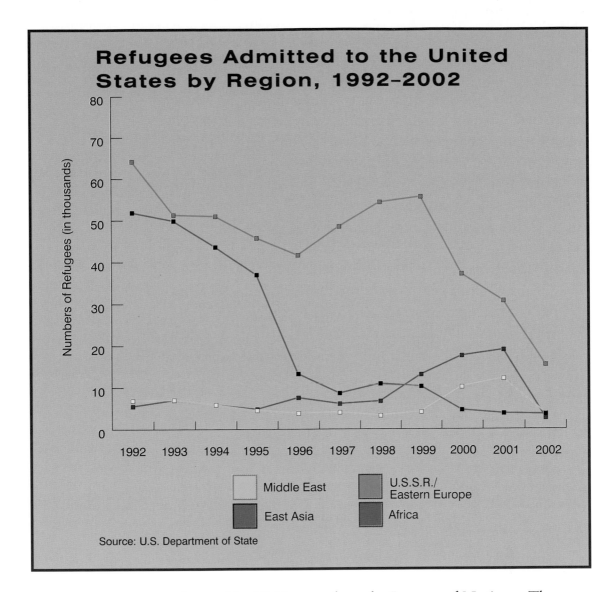

Refugees Admitted to the United States by Region, 1992–2002

Numbers of Refugees (in thousands)

Middle East

East Asia

U.S.S.R./ Eastern Europe

Africa

Source: U.S. Department of State

was formed in 1945 to replace the League of Nations. The IRO's constitution guaranteed assistance to specially designated groups of refugees. Victims of the Nazi regime and orphans under the age of 16 were among those the IRO focused on repatriating or resettling. After the war, the organization helped a number of European refugees to go back to their own countries, though most of them had to resettle in other countries. The United States accepted over 30 percent of the more than one million people resettled by the IRO.

The IRO was designed to be temporary and so was terminated

in 1952. During the period of the IRO's service, the UN councils recognized the need for a more permanent agency to help the world's refugees. The 1948 Universal Declaration of Human Rights, drawn up by the UN Commission on Human Rights, included an article that stated, "Everyone has the right to seek and to enjoy in other countries asylum from persecution." In 1950, the agency of the United Nations High Commissioner for Refugees (UNHCR) was established. The UNHCR was designated as a non-partisan organization, headed by a leader also called the High Commissioner. Its first major mission was to help those who were made refugees by World War II. In July 1951, at a conference in Geneva, Switzerland, 26 nations adopted the Convention Relating to the Status of Refugees, a document that became the legal framework for UNHCR.

The Convention was much more detailed than any previous decisions relating to the classification and treatment of refugees. It defined a refugee as follows:

> [Any person who] . . . owing to well-founded fear of being persecuted for reasons of race, religion, nationality, membership of a particular social group or political opinion, is outside the country of his nationality and is unable or, owing to such fear, is unwilling to avail himself of the protection of that country; or who, not having a nationality and being outside the country of his former habitual residence . . . is unable or, owing to such fear, is unwilling to return to it.

The Convention also introduced the principle of *non-refoulement*, which committed governments not to turn refugees back to a home territory where their lives would be endangered or where they would be persecuted. This important principle has been part of refugee law ever since the 1951 Convention, although its application has not always been clear. The Convention did not specifically offer protection for internally displaced persons (IDPs).

After the 1951 Geneva Convention

Although the Geneva Convention was an essential step forward in the protection of refugees, it had many limitations. For instance, only those who had become refugees "as a result of events occurring before 1 January 1951" were considered "Convention Refugees." In other words, the Convention only served Europeans who had become refugees because of World War II. Originally, the founders of UNHCR and the Convention thought that they would only need to give major assistance to refugees for a few years, anticipating that the refugee problem would be resolved in that time. But during the 15 years that followed the Convention, major refugee crises arose elsewhere, especially in Africa. UNHCR was still able to help these people, but the specifications of the 1951 Convention were much too narrow to be applied directly to all refugee situations. Many countries realized that the Convention had to be extended so as to help a greater number of people.

In 1967, the UN passed the Protocol to the 1951 Convention that removed the pre-1951 time limit in the refugee definition. By the end of the 1990s, over 130 states had accepted the Protocol, which includes the provisions of the Convention. The Protocol was not the final international agreement on the status of refugees, as the situations facing refugees have since changed frequently. Although there has not been another world

Resettling African Refugees

Until recently, North America has not been a major destination for African refugees. Most of them had gone to refugee camps in other parts of Africa, or to other parts of the Western world, such as Europe. In the last few years, though, many African refugees have been resettled in the United States and Canada. In 1998, the United States only resettled about 7,000 African refugees. In the year 2000, the number had increased to 18,000 refugees from 25 different African countries. In 2002, the United States agreed to take a segment of the 12,000 Somali Bantus, members of an ethnic minority group who had been refugees since the early 1990s. However, in that year only 2,566 refugees from Africa actually were admitted to America in 2002. Most of the African refugees who have resettled in the United States come from Ethiopia, Liberia, Somalia, and Sudan.

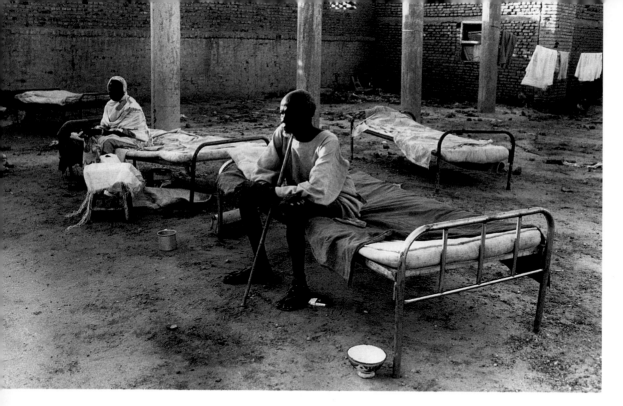

war for over 50 years, refugee crises have continued to develop around the world for all kinds of reasons. There were 6.5 million more displaced people worldwide at the end of the 1990s than when the decade began, according to the World Refugee Survey 2000. Each refugee crisis has presented its own challenges, and since documents such as the 1951 Convention and the 1967 Protocol cannot apply to all situations, governments and organizations in different parts of the world have responded by drawing up agreements that fit local circumstances.

One such agreement was the Convention Governing the Specific Aspects of Refugee Problems in Africa, adopted by the Organization of African Unity (OAU) in 1969. One important distinction in this convention was that people could now become refugees as a result of disturbances or conflicts caused by "external aggression, occupation, [or] foreign domination." Another regional agreement was the 1984 Cartagena Declaration, made in response to the refugee crisis of the 1980s in Central America. Refugees had emerged in that region because of civil wars in Nicaragua, El Salvador, and

Sudanese refugees take shelter after fleeing civil war in the country's southern region in 1988. In recent decades the United States and Canada have accepted large groups of refugees from African countries where war and persecution are most prevalent.

Guatemala. Representatives from Mexico and Panama had adopted the declaration, which stated that people could claim refugee status as a result of "circumstances which have seriously disturbed public order." These and other new agreements made the 1951 Convention and the 1967 Protocol more inclusive to refugees, opening up possibilities to help victims in different parts of the world.

Although the Convention and the Protocol have greatly affected refugees around the world, there remain many countries that have never adopted these agreements. And even the countries that have adopted the Convention and the Protocol have applied them in very different ways. It is thus often difficult for policy makers of different countries to reach a common ground on international refugee law.

Officially, UNHCR is still not a permanent organization. Many people continue to envision a resolution to the refugee problem. At present, the mandate for UNHCR is renewed every five years. Although it does more work than any other organization to help refugees, it relies completely on donations from governments, private organizations, and individuals.

The United States and Canada have been leaders in refugee protection for decades. The United States has accepted more refugees than any other country, and Canada has accepted more than most other Western nations. These two countries have benefited from important contributions made by refugees, yet there also have been refugee crises and changes on the world scene that have forced the governments to rethink their refugee policies.

2 REFUGEE POLICY THROUGH THE YEARS

The United States and Canada were founded by immigrants. Except for the native peoples, who have been in North America for thousands of years, few people in the United States or Canada can trace the history of their family on the continent back for more than a few centuries. Most families have been in these two countries for a much shorter period than that.

Today, the United States and Canada lead the world in accepting and assisting refugees. Between 1975 and 1999, more than 2.3 million refugees resettled in the United States. During that period, the rest of the world's countries combined did not accept as many refugees for resettlement. Canada received the first-ever Nansen Medal in 1986 as a tribute to its refugee programs. In the 1990s, Canada accepted more refugees in relation to its general population than any other country.

With their advanced resettlement programs, the United States and Canada attract a great many refugees. In 2002, a Somali refugee awaiting resettlement in the United States said: "Going to America is a dream. It is the choice between the fire and paradise." UNHCR has said that Canada's refugee program is "in many ways a model of fairness and due process." However, the American and Canadian refugee programs have also received criticism. Some say the governments could do more to help people in need; others say that even in periods of stability the number of refugees accepted each year (generally

◀Immigrants wait to pass through customs at New York City's Ellis Island, 1905. Refugees who resettle in the United States and Canada join the millions of immigrants who arrive looking for personal freedoms they might not have had in their own countries.

over 70,000 a year in the United States) is too high. As neighbors and allies, the United States and Canada have often taken similar approaches to the refugee problem. They have worked together, coordinating on such things as the movement of refugees between the two countries. But they have also sometimes taken different approaches to refugees. To understand these and other policy differences, it is necessary to briefly examine the history of immigration and refugee policy in the United States and Canada.

A Short History of U.S. Immigration

Immigration to the United States has been characterized by openness punctuated by periods of restriction. During the 17th, 18th, and 19th centuries, immigration was essentially open without restriction, and, at times, immigrants were even recruited to come to America. Between 1783 and 1820, approximately 250,000 immigrants arrived at U.S. shores. Between 1841 and 1860, more than 4 million immigrants came; most were from England, Ireland, and Germany.

Historically, race and ethnicity have played a role in legislation to restrict immigration. The Chinese Exclusion Act of 1882, which was not repealed until 1943, specifically prevented Chinese people from becoming U.S. citizens and did not allow Chinese laborers to immigrate for the next decade. An agreement with Japan in the early 1900s prevented most Japanese immigration to the United States.

Until the 1920s, no numerical restrictions on immigration existed in the United States, although health restrictions applied. The only other significant restrictions came in 1917, when passing a literacy test became a requirement for immigrants. Presidents Cleveland, Taft, and Wilson had vetoed similar measures earlier. In addition, in 1917 a prohibition was added to the law against the immigration of people from Asia (defined as the Asiatic barred zone). While a few of these prohibitions were lifted during World War II, they were not repealed until 1952, and even then Asians were only allowed in under very small annual quotas.

A political cartoon published in 1921 satirizes the strict quota on the number of European immigrants who could enter the United States. Only a tiny percent of people of a certain nationality were allowed in the country. This quota remained in place in the years before and during World War II, when many Eastern Europeans hoping to escape Nazi persecution were denied entry.

U.S. Immigration Policy from World War I to 1965

During World War I, the federal government required that all travelers to the United States obtain a visa at a U.S. consulate or diplomatic post abroad. As former State Department consular affairs officer C. D. Scully points out, by making that requirement permanent Congress, by 1924, established the framework of temporary, or non-immigrant visas (for study, work, or travel), and immigrant visas (for permanent residence). That framework remains in place today.

After World War I, cultural intolerance and bizarre racial

theories led to new immigration restrictions. The House
Judiciary Committee employed a eugenics consultant, Dr.
Harry N. Laughlin, who asserted that certain races were inferi-
or. Another leader of the eugenics movement, Madison Grant,
argued that Jews, Italians, and others were inferior because of
their supposedly different skull size.

The Immigration Act of 1924, preceded by the Temporary
Quota Act of 1921, set new numerical limits on immigration
based on "national origin." Taking effect in 1929, the 1924 act
set annual quotas on immigrants that were specifically designed
to keep out southern Europeans, such as Italians and Greeks.
Generally no more than 100 people of the proscribed nationalities were permitted to immigrate.

While the new law was rigid, the U.S. Department of State's
restrictive interpretation directed consular officers overseas to
be even stricter in their application of the "public charge" pro-
vision. (A public charge is someone unable to support himself
or his family.) As author Laura Fermi wrote, "In response to
the new cry for restriction at the beginning of the [Great
Depression] . . . the consuls were to interpret very strictly the
clause prohibiting admission of aliens 'likely to become public
charges; and to deny the visa to an applicant who in their opinion might become a public charge at any time.'"

In the early 1900s, more than one million immigrants a year
came to the United States. In 1930—the first year of the
national-origin quotas—approximately 241,700 immigrants
were admitted. But under the State Department's strict interpre-
tations, only 23,068 immigrants entered during 1933, the
smallest total since 1831. Later these restrictions prevented
many Jews in Germany and elsewhere in Europe from escaping
what would become the Holocaust. At the height of the
Holocaust in 1943, the United States admitted fewer than
6,000 refugees.

The Displaced Persons Act of 1948, the nation's first refugee
law, allowed many refugees from World War II to settle in the
United States. The law put into place policy changes that had

already seen immigration rise from 38,119 in 1945 to 108,721 in 1946 (and later to 249,187 in 1950). One-third of those admitted between 1948 and 1951 were Poles, with ethnic Germans forming the second-largest group.

The 1952 Immigration and Nationality Act is best known for its restrictions against those who supported communism or anarchy. However, the bill's other provisions were quite restrictive and were passed over the veto of President Truman. The 1952 act retained the national-origin quota system for the Eastern Hemisphere. The Western Hemisphere continued to operate without a quota and relied on other qualitative factors to limit immigration. Moreover, during that time, the Mexican bracero program, from 1942 to 1964, allowed millions of Mexican agricultural workers to work temporarily in the United States.

The 1952 act set aside half of each national quota to be divided among three preference categories for relatives of U.S. citizens and permanent residents. The other half went to aliens with high education or exceptional abilities. These quotas applied only to those from the Eastern Hemisphere.

A Halt to the National-Origin Quotas

The Immigration and Nationality Act of 1965 became a landmark in immigration legislation by specifically striking the racially based national-origin quotas. It removed the barriers to Asian immigration, which later led to opportunities to immigrate for many Filipinos, Chinese, Koreans, and others. The Western Hemisphere was designated a ceiling of 120,000 immigrants but without a preference system or per country limits. Modifications made in 1978 ultimately combined the Western and Eastern Hemispheres into one preference system and one ceiling of 290,000.

The 1965 act built on the existing system—without the national-origin quotas—and gave somewhat more priority to family relationships. It did not completely overturn the existing system but rather carried forward essentially intact the family immigration categories from the 1959 amendments to the Immigration and Nationality Act. Even though the text of the law prior to 1965 indicated that half of the immigration slots were reserved for skilled employment immigration, in practice, Immigration and Naturalization Service (INS) statistics show that 86 percent of the visas issued between 1952 and 1965 went for family immigration.

A number of significant pieces of legislation since 1980 have shaped the current immigration system. First, the Refugee Act of 1980 removed refugees from the annual world limit and established that the president would set the number of refugees

North America's First Refugees

The arrival of refugees is not a new development in American and Canadian history. Starting in the 1600s, and over the next three centuries, many of the people who arrived on the shores of North America were fleeing religious or political persecution; others were fleeing famine or extreme poverty. During this time, people even moved across the border between the United States and Canada, in both directions.

Some of the earliest arrivals in the future United States were Puritans. This Christian group disagreed with the practices of the Church of England. Because of their criticism of the Church, they became victims of prejudice and discrimination in England, and could not freely practice their faith. Some of the Puritans left for Holland, a move that did not improve their situation a great deal. In 1620, a group of Puritans sailed from Holland to Massachusetts aboard the *Mayflower*. Other Puritans arrived in New England over the next few decades.

In the 1750s, the British and the French were fighting for domination of the Canadian colonies. The British colonialists viewed the French inhabitants of Acadia, a region on the east coast, as a threat to their interests in Canada. In 1755, the British tried to force the Acadians to take an oath of their allegiance. The Acadians declined, and the British forces responded by declaring them "non-citizens." More than 10,000 Acadian peasants were then forced to leave their homes and go to the American colonies. The British general in charge of removing the Acadians described the operation as "a Scene of Woe and Diestress." British soldiers destroyed the peasants' farms and houses so that there would be nowhere for who could be admitted each year after consultations with Congress.

Second, the 1986 Immigration Reform and Control Act (IRCA) introduced sanctions against employers who "knowingly" hired undocumented immigrants (those here illegally). It also provided amnesty for many undocumented immigrants.

Third, the Immigration Act of 1990 increased legal immigration by 40 percent. In particular, the act significantly increased the number of employment-based immigrants (to 140,000), while also boosting family immigration.

Fourth, the 1996 Illegal Immigration Reform and Immigrant

them to go if they escaped. Some of the Acadians went to the French colony in Louisiana, while others went to New England. Eventually, a number of the exiles returned home.

During the American Revolution, or War of Independence (1775–83), rebels fought for independence from Britain. Up to 500,000 people living in the American colonies did not support the rebels and continued to support British rule. The Loyalists faced discrimination because of their politics and their religious beliefs. Many of them lost their houses and properties. About 50,000 Loyalists left the United States for Canada, the largest wave departing after the American victory. Many Loyalists were originally from England, but there were also Scottish, Dutch, German, and Jewish Loyalists. In Canada, they settled in areas such as Nova Scotia and Ontario. A Loyalist memorial in Nova Scotia bears the inscription: "They sacrificed everything save honour."

In the decades before the abolition of slavery in 1865, there were millions of black slaves living in the United States, a large number of whom refused to accept a lifetime of slavery. Between 1786 and the 1865, black refugees fled to freedom in Canada by means of the Underground Railroad, a network of houses and routes run by people willing to help the slaves. Many escaped slaves did not make it. However, about 40,000 slaves reached Canada through the Underground Railroad. After the end of the Civil War (1861–65), about half of these refugees returned to the United States.

Responsibility Act (IIRAIRA) significantly tightened rules that permitted undocumented immigrants to convert to legal status and made other changes that tightened immigration law in areas such as political asylum and deportation.

Fifth, in response to the September 11, 2001, terrorist attacks, the USA PATRIOT Act and the Enhanced Border Security and Visa Entry Reform Act tightened rules on the granting of visas to individuals from certain countries and enhanced the federal government's monitoring and detention authority over foreign nationals in the United States.

New U.S. Immigration Agencies

In a dramatic reorganization of the federal government, the Homeland Security Act of 2002 abolished the Immigration and Naturalization Service and transferred its immigration service and enforcement functions from the Department of Justice into a new Department of Homeland Security. The Customs Service, the Coast Guard, and parts of other agencies were also transferred into the new department.

The Department of Homeland Security, with regards to immigration, is organized as follows: The Bureau of Customs and Border Protection (BCBP) contains Customs and Immigration inspectors, who check the documents of travelers to the United States at air, sea, and land ports of entry; and Border Patrol agents, the uniformed agents who seek to prevent unlawful entry along the southern and northern border. The new Bureau of Immigration and Customs Enforcement (BICE) employs investigators, who attempt to find undocumented immigrants inside the United States, and Detention and Removal officers, who detain and seek to deport such individuals. The new Bureau of Citizenship and Immigration Services (BCIS) is where people go, or correspond with, to become U.S. citizens or obtain permission to work or extend their stay in the United States.

President George W. Bush signs the Enhanced Border Security and Visa Entry Reform Act with congressional members in attendance, May 2002. The act, along with the USA PATRIOT Act, was passed in response to the September 2001 terrorist attacks.

Following the terrorist attacks of September 11, 2001, the Department of Justice adopted several measures that did not require new legislation to be passed by Congress. Some of these measures created controversy and raised concerns about civil liberties. For example, FBI and INS agents detained for months more than 1,000 foreign nationals of Middle Eastern descent and refused to release the names of the individuals. It is alleged that the Department of Justice adopted tactics that discouraged the detainees from obtaining legal assistance. The Department of Justice also began requiring foreign nationals from primarily Muslim nations to be fingerprinted and questioned by immigration officers upon entry or if they have been living in the United States. Those involved in the September 11 attacks were not immigrants—people who become permanent residents with a right to stay in the United States—but holders of temporary visas, primarily visitor or tourist visas.

A Pakastani man passes through the Islamabad International Airport after being deported from the United States in July 2003. A group of Muslims was deported after September 11, 2001, for being in the country illegally.

Immigration to the United States Today

Today, the annual rate of legal immigration is lower than that at earlier periods in U.S. history. For example, from 1901 to 1910 approximately 10.4 immigrants per 1,000 U.S. residents came to the United States. Today, the annual rate is about 3.5 immigrants per 1,000 U.S. residents. While the percentage of foreign-born people in the U.S. population has risen above 11 percent, it remains lower than the 13 percent or higher that prevailed in the country from 1860 to 1930. Still, as has been the case previously in U.S. history, some people argue that even legal immigration should be lowered. These people maintain that immigrants take jobs native-born Americans could fill and that U.S. population growth, which immigration contributes to, harms the environment. In 1996 Congress voted against efforts to reduce legal immigration.

Most immigrants (800,000 to one million annually) enter the United States legally. But over the years the undocumented (illegal) portion of the population has increased to about 2.8 percent of the U.S. population—approximately 8 million people in all.

Today, the legal immigration system in the United States contains many rules, permitting only individuals who fit into certain categories to immigrate—and in many cases only after waiting anywhere from 1 to 10 years or more, depending on

The Melting Pot of America

A conventional metaphor for American society is the "melting pot." The image symbolizes America's inclusiveness, as well as the assimilation expected of different cultures to help form a national culture. The "melting pot" expression originally comes from the title of a 1908 play by Israel Zangwill, a British writer and son of Russian immigrants. In the play, a Russian-Jewish composer named David Quixano wants to write a symphony about his new country, the United States. He sees America as "a divinely appointed crucible in which all the ethnic division of mankind will . . . become fused into one group, signifying the brotherhood of man."

the demand in that category. The system, representing a compromise among family, employment, and human rights concerns, has the following elements:

A U.S. citizen may sponsor for immigration a spouse, parent, sibling, or minor or adult child.

A lawful permanent resident (green card holder) may sponsor only a spouse or child.

A foreign national may immigrate if he or she gains an employer sponsor.

An individual who can show that he or she has a "well-founded fear of persecution" may come to the country as a refugee—or be allowed to stay as an asylee (someone who receives asylum).

Beyond these categories, essentially the only other way to immigrate is to apply for and receive one of the "diversity" visas, which are granted annually by lottery to those from "underrepresented" countries.

In 1996 changes to the law prohibited nearly all incoming immigrants from being eligible for federal public benefits, such as welfare, during their first five years in the country. Refugees were mostly excluded from these changes. In addition, families who sponsor relatives must sign an affidavit of support showing they can financially take care of an immigrant who falls on hard times.

A Short History of Canadian Immigration

In the 1800s, immigration into Canada was largely unrestricted. Farmers and artisans from England and Ireland made up a significant portion of 19th-century immigrants. England's Parliament passed laws that facilitated and encouraged the voyage to North America, particularly for the poor.

After the United States barred Chinese railroad workers from settling in the country, Canada encouraged the immigration of Chinese laborers to assist in the building of Canadian railways. Responding to the racial views of the time, the Canadian Parliament began charging a "head tax" for Chinese and South

Asian (Indian) immigrants in 1885. The fee of $50—later raised to $500—was well beyond the means of laborers making one or two dollars a day. Later, the government sought additional ways to prohibit Asians from entering the country. For example, it decided to require a "continuous journey," meaning that immigrants to Canada had to travel from their country on a boat that made an uninterrupted passage. For immigrants or asylum seekers from Asia this was nearly impossible.

As the 20th century progressed, concerns about race led to further restrictions on immigration to Canada. These restrictions particularly hurt Jewish and other refugees seeking to flee persecution in Europe. Government statistics indicate that Canada accepted no more than 5,000 Jewish refugees before and during the Holocaust.

After World War II, Canada, like the United States, began accepting thousands of Europeans displaced by the war. Canada's laws were modified to accept these war refugees, as well as Hungarians fleeing Communist authorities after the crushing of the 1956 Hungarian Revolution.

Lester Pearson, prime minister of Canada from 1963 to 1968, believed that immigrants were key to the country's economic growth. In 1966 the Canadian government introduced a statement stressing the importance of an open immigration policy.

The Immigration Act of 1952 in Canada allowed for a "tap on, tap off" approach to immigration, granting administrative authorities the power to allow more immigrants into the country in good economic times, and fewer in times of recession. The shortcoming of such an approach is that there is little evidence immigrants harm a national economy and much evidence they contribute to economic growth, particularly in the growth of the labor force.

In 1966 the government of Prime Minister Lester Pearson introduced a policy statement stressing how immigrants were key to Canada's economic growth. With Canada's relatively small population base, it became clear that in the absence of newcomers, the country would not be able to grow. The policy was introduced four years after Parliament enacted important legislation that eliminated Canada's own version of racially based national-origin quotas.

In 1967 a new law established a points system that awarded entry to potential immigrants using criteria based primarily on an individual's age, language ability, skills, education, family relationships, and job prospects. The total points needed for entry of an immigrant is set by the Minister of Citizenship and Immigration Canada. The new law also established a category for humanitarian (refugee) entry.

The 1976 Immigration Act refined and expanded the possibility for entry under the points system, particularly for those seeking to sponsor family members. The act also expanded refugee and asylum law to comport with Canada's international obligations. The law established five basic categories for immigration into Canada: 1) family; 2) humanitarian; 3) independents (including skilled workers), who immigrate to Canada on their own; 4) assisted relatives; and 5) business immigrants (including investors, entrepreneurs, and the self-employed).

The new Immigration and Refugee Protection Act, which took effect June 28, 2002, made a series of modifications to existing Canadian immigration law. The act, and the regulations that followed, toughened rules on those seeking asylum and the process for removing people unlawfully in Canada.

The law modified the points system, adding greater flexibility for skilled immigrants and temporary workers to become permanent residents, and evaluating skilled workers on the weight of their transferable skills as well as those of their specific occupation. The legislation also made it easier for employers to have a labor shortage declared in an industry or sector, which would facilitate the entry of foreign workers in that industry or sector.

On family immigration, the act permitted parents to sponsor dependent children up to the age of 22 (previously 19 was the maximum age at which a child could be sponsored for immigration). The act also allowed partners in common-law arrangements, including same-sex partners, to be considered as family members for the purpose of immigration sponsorship. Along with these liberalizing measures, the act also included provisions to address perceived gaps in immigration-law enforcement.

A Closer Look at Refugee Policy

Although both nations have done a great service to refugees—since World War II, in particular—there have been occasions when their commitment fell short. The most famous of these incidents occurred in 1939.

In 1939, at the start of World War II, hundreds of Jewish refugees aboard the SS *St. Louis* tried to enter Cuba. When their entry documents to Cuba were canceled, they turned toward the United States. As the ship passed near Miami, Florida, the passengers were close enough to hear the music being played in hotels along the waterfront. However, they were not allowed entry and so had to return to Europe, where they faced persecution and even death. Canada also did not offer assistance to the refugees.

Eight years after the *St. Louis* incident, Congress passed the Displaced Persons Act, the first U.S. law to deal specifically with refugees. In the 1950s and 1960s, Congress passed more acts to help refugees. Under the 1952 McCarran-Walter Act, the U.S. Attorney General had the authority to let unlimited numbers of refugees enter the country temporarily. The 1953 Refugee Relief Act and the 1957 Refugee-Escapee Act gave refugee status to people escaping Middle Eastern countries and communist countries in Eastern Europe. In 1968, the United States accepted the 1967 Protocol to the 1951 United Nations Convention Relating to the Status of Refugees, an important development because the U.S. had originally not accepted the Geneva Convention.

Between 1975 and 1980, large numbers of refugees started arriving in the United States from Vietnam and other Southeast Asian countries. Because of its involvement in the Vietnam War (1957–75), the United States felt responsibility and sympathy for these war victims and saw a need for improved refugee policies. In 1979 Joseph Califano, the U.S. Secretary of the Department of Health and Human Services, pled for the government to allow more of these refugees in the country. He stated: "By our choice on this issue, we reveal to the world—and more importantly to ourselves—whether we truly live by our ideals or simply carve them on our monuments." A year later, Congress passed the Refugee Act of 1980.

The Refugee Act recognized how the situation of refugees differs from that of immigrants in that refugees are forced to leave their countries instead of choosing freely. The new law also recognized asylees, people who apply for special status *after* they have already arrived in the country, either legally or illegally. Finally, the act established a detailed resettlement program for refugees in the United States that had not existed before, and today it remains the most important law concerning the status of refugees in the United States. Since the act's passage, more American organizations have worked toward helping refugees in the world at large. In 1989 a national branch of UNHCR, USA for UNHCR, was established. This volunteer organization raises money and awareness for the UN agency.

South Vietnamese refugees aboard a sailboat leave the country after North Vietnamese forces invade the city of Saigon, April 1975. U.S. Congress passed the Refugee Act of 1980 to better address the plight of Vietnamese war refugees and other individuals forced to leave their countries.

After September 11

After the terrorist attacks of September 2001, refugees were among those most severely affected. For two months, the U.S. government suspended its refugee resettlement program, and as a result 20,000 refugees suddenly could not enter the country. One of the results of the program's suspension was that fewer refugees were admitted to the U.S. than in any year since 1987, according to the World Refugee Survey 2002, issued by the U.S. Committee for Refugees. The United States admitted only 27,075 refugees in 2002, less than two and a half times the number of refugees admitted in any of the previous 10 years.

An additional reason that fewer refugees were admitted in 2002 was that they faced new procedures after the September 11 attacks. A series of security enhancements were added to help prevent fraud or the entry of those who could be a national security threat to the United States. In the long run, these enhancements will likely benefit the U.S. refugee program, since it would remove the argument from potential critics that refugees are not sufficiently screened and hence are security threats. On the other hand, the new procedures, including extensive name checks against U.S. law enforcement databases, verification of family relationships, and the fingerprinting of refugees, has significantly slowed the processing of refugees and resulted in far fewer admissions. In 2003, U.S. refugee admissions still had not recovered, prompting concern among refugee advocates and members of Congress.

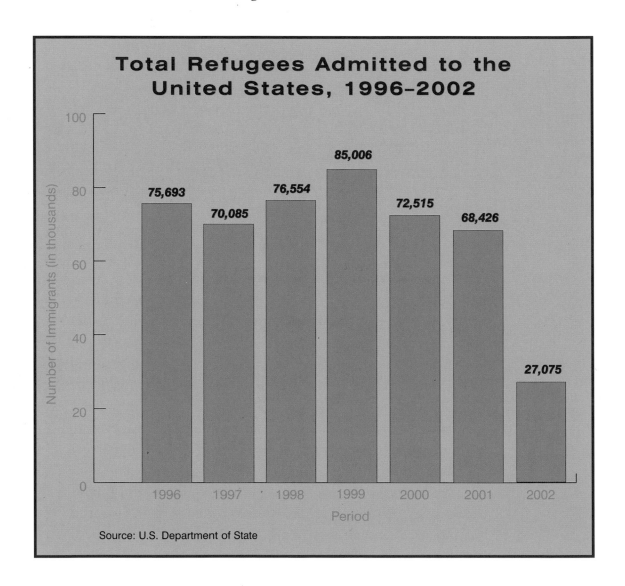

Total Refugees Admitted to the United States, 1996–2002

Source: U.S. Department of State

Understanding U.S. Refugee and Asylee Law

Refugees and asylees both must have a "well-founded fear of persecution," but under U.S. law there is a difference between the two groups. Generally speaking, a refugee is someone who is interviewed *outside* the United States and an asylee is interviewed *inside* the country.

While the term *refugee* is often used for both groups of people, this distinction is important. An asylum seeker—someone who wants to become an asylee—may come to the United States on a tourist visa, or even use fake documents. He or she will then will request asylum either affirmatively, by going to a government immigration office, or will ask for asylum as a defense against being deported from the country. If an asylum officer does not approve that claim, the asylum seeker can go before an immigration judge for a final decision. If the person is in custody and seeking to avoid being deported, an immigration judge, rather than an asylum officer, will hear the case first. Under its international commitments, neither the United States nor Canada will deport an individual who will be tortured in their home country; however, some individuals who have committed serious criminal offenses or who represent a national security threat may be denied asylum.

The Bureau of Population, Refugees, and Migration (PRM) in the U.S. Department of State takes a leading role on U.S. refugee policy in partnership with the Bureau of Citizenship and Immigration Services (BCIS) and the Office of Refugee Resettlement in the Department of Health and Human Services (HHS). In addition to managing funds appropriated by Congress to relieve humanitarian and refugee crises overseas, a primary mission of the PRM bureau is set policy guidelines for the refugee admissions program. These guidelines govern who should be eligible for interviews, what the priorities are for those interviews, and how refugees who are admitted should be resettled. (American refugee organizations, often religiously affiliated, try to coordinate with the PRM bureau to establish resettlement guidelines.)

Every year, PRM, in coordination with other federal agencies, prepares a report with recommendations for how many individuals from each region of the world should be admitted in the next fiscal year. Ultimately, however, it is the president, in consultation with Congress, who decides on the worldwide refugee "ceiling" for the year. Each year the secretary of state or another Cabinet-level official meet with the leaders of the House and Senate judiciary committees to discuss the refugee admission numbers. While there is usually some give-and-take, the administration's initial proposal has traditionally been the same as the final number that the president usually announces prior to the beginning of the next fiscal year.

Interviews are conducted overseas not by the State Department but by refugee adjudicators, or interviewers, who are part of the BCIS. These adjudicators must assess the credibility of the person sitting before them by weighing his or her answers to questions and examining documents he or she may present. Voluntary agencies, usually U.S.–based refugee organizations under contract to the government, may assist refugees in preparing their cases. UNHCR will generally act as a "gate-keeper" and refer several thousand individuals a year as

A Jamaican woman waits in line at the Florida District office of the Bureau of Citizenship and Immigration Services (BCIS), 2003. The BCIS, which replaced the Immigration and Naturalization Service (INS), has aimed to make the immigrant processing system more efficient.

prospects for resettlement in the United States.

Since there are so many refugees to select for interviews, the State Department has established a priority system. Priority 1 (P-1) status is given to refugees whose need for resettlement is very high. Priority 2 (P-2) is for "specific groups (within certain nationalities)" of special concern. Other priority levels are based on relationship with a U.S. family member. Although having a relationship with a U.S. citizen or lawful permanent resident is an interview priority, it is not sufficient for gaining refugee status—the individual still must show he or she has a legitimate reason for fearing persecution. Although many people receive refugee status every year, PRM still receives criticism for setting interview criteria that are too restrictive and thus prevent legitimate refugees from even having the opportunity to present their cases.

Those who are granted refugee status can work in the United States. After living in the country for one year, they can apply to stay permanently, and after five years, they can usually apply for U.S. citizenship. Refugees can receive medical help and other types of special assistance right away, while other immigrants have to wait five years to become eligible for these benefits. Asylees are also authorized to work after being granted asylum, but the BCIS is only allowed to grant permanent residence to 10,000 asylees every year, a restriction that has created waiting periods of five years or longer for green cards.

The work of the BCIS and related organizations is not easy. They must decide as fairly as possible who is really eligible for refugee status, and which cases are the most urgent. Doris Meissner, former commissioner of the INS, stated in 1999 that the organization was far more professional than it was before, and that it processed applications "faster, more equitably and more humanely than at any other time." As the BCIS tries to improve on the track record of the INS, keeping the best interests of both the refugees and the American people in mind, it is pressed to make difficult decisions every day.

Canadian Refugee Policy

After World War II, Canadian refugee policy improved and the country resettled many refugees from countries such as Hungary and Czechoslovakia. Although the Canadian government most eagerly accepted young, skilled refugees, it also sought to help many simply on the grounds that their lives were in danger. Still, refugees did not have many basic rights in Canada until 1969, when the Canadian government accepted the Geneva Convention and its 1967 Protocol.

During the 1970s, changes in refugee policy allowed for Canada to accept refugees at a growing rate. Refugees were placed in a specially designated class that was exempt from the immigration points system. The pivotal 1976 Immigration Act—implemented in 1978—established the Refugee Status Advisory Committee (RSAC), which was responsible for looking at refugee claims in detail. This act recognized that refugees did not always fit the standard classification and that new refugee categories should be created whenever necessary.

The Canadian government took a controversial step in 2000 when it eliminated the Right of Landing Fee (ROLF) for refugees. In existence since 1995, the ROLF helps cover the costs of programs for people who have just arrived in Canada. When the decision was announced, Elinor Caplan, the Minister of Citizenship and Immigration, said: "Refugees have already faced enormous difficulties and stresses. By eliminating this fee we help them to get on with their lives and to integrate successfully into Canadian society." Some people felt that this decision was unfair, since other immigrants continued to pay the ROLF.

Canada's partnership with the United States has greatly influenced the legislation of certain refugee laws. In October 2002, the two governments signed the Safe Third Country Agreement, which stated that asylum claims should be made in the first country of arrival. In the past, many asylum seekers had arrived in the United States but then continued on to the Canadian border to take advantage of Canada's services to newcomers. Some estimates say that 75 percent of the people seeking asylum in

Canada had arrived to the United States first. Under this new law, however, Canada will not accept an asylum seeker who has arrived in the United States and traveled to Canada.

Defenders of the Safe Third Country Agreement argue that once people have reached a safe country, they should remain there. Officials and some refugee advocacy groups feared that the new law would push refugees to start trying to cross the border illegally. As a gesture of compromise, Canada agreed that it would resettle up to 200 refugees a year who were officially referred to them by the United States. The U.S. government also adopted a policy of allowing those asylum seekers with relatives in the United States to apply for asylum there.

The refugee admittance process in Canada is similar to the American process. Canadian immigration officials go to refugee camps and other places, conduct interviews of potential refugees, and offer refugee status to selected individuals. Commonly, refugees are found outside their country of citizenship, placing them in the "Convention Refugees Abroad" class.

Refugees who are found in their country of citizenship are placed in the "Source Country" class, and the immigration process is relatively easy for this group. Immediately upon arriving, they are granted permanent residence status, and after living in Canada for three years, they can apply for Canadian citizenship. As well as being sponsored by the government, they may receive help from private sponsors and local organizations. Some of the Sudanese refugees who emerged in the 1980s resettled in British Columbia, where the province's Immigration Services Society helped them find employment and a place to live.

Canada stands as an international leader in the practice of refugee protection. According to Adrienne Clarkson, the governor general of Canada since 2000 and a former refugee from Hong Kong, "Canada has a great track record for giving, and I would like us to continue to be committed to it forever. . . . I think we have to do even more than our share, because we have so much more."

3 THE BOAT PEOPLE

Vietnam, Cambodia, and Laos are Southeast Asian countries that are located south of China and east of Thailand. Together, these three nations are known as Indochina. Since 1975, more than 2 million Indochinese refugees have fled their countries and resettled in other parts of the world. The United States alone has taken more than 1.2 million of these refugees. Canada has accepted over 100,000 refugees from Vietnam and thousands more from other Indochinese countries. This refugee crisis stemmed from developments in Indochina over the past several decades.

The Vietnam War and the Indochinese Refugees

Vietnam was a French colony from the mid-19th century until World War II. During the war, Japan gained control of Vietnam, but had lost possession of the country along with its other major losses toward the end of the war. In the post-World War II period, communist forces within Vietnam fought to free the country from the control of France. In 1954, Vietnam was divided into North Vietnam and South Vietnam, with a communist government in the north and a non-communist government in the south. During the 1950s and 1960s, a guerrilla communist group in South Vietnam called the Viet Cong fought to overthrow the government. The Viet Cong relied greatly on the military assistance of the North Vietnamese forces.

◀ Two Indochinese refugees float in a small sailboat off the coast of Thailand, 1990. Since 1975, war and political repression in Vietnam, Cambodia, and Laos have produced over 2 million Indochinese refugees, also known as "boat people." The United States and Canada have accepted over 1.3 million boat people.

Following World War II, the U.S. government developed an anti-communist policy that extended into the 1950s and the following decades. In Indochina, the government decided to carry on where France had left off in fighting communism. Between 1965 and 1968, U.S. forces in Vietnam increased from about 25,000 to 500,000. After 1968, with much opposition to the war at home, the United States had decided it suffered too many casualties and slowly began withdrawing its troops from Indochina. However, the war continued and, in 1970, spilled over into neighboring Cambodia.

The Vietnam War, which had claimed the lives of over one million people, ended in 1975, when the North Vietnamese

Smoke rises from firebombed buildings in Saigon after the Viet Cong launched the Tet Offensive, a major battle of the Vietnam War, January 1968. The war, which ended in 1975, produced hundreds of thousands of refugees.

government took over the entire country. A number of refugees had gone to the United States and other parts of the world before the end of the war. In 1975, many Americans wanted to put the many wounds of the Vietnam War behind them, but the refugee crisis had only just begun.

Vietnam was in ruins after years of battles and bombing campaigns. The people of South Vietnam were also afraid of political persecution under the new communist government. Communist forces conquered several South Vietnamese cities, and many inhabitants of these cities fled for safety. Many Cambodians also fled the persecution of their communist government, which had begun a reign of terror in 1975.

April 1975 was a pivotal month in the U.S. response to the growing refugee crisis. Even before the South Vietnamese city of Saigon fell to the Communists on April 30 and ended the war, the U.S. government was taking steps to help Indochinese refugees, as well as those who were about to become refugees. President Gerald Ford called the refugee crisis "a tragedy unbelievable in its ramifications." On April 4, Operation Baby Lift was launched. This program brought 2,000 Vietnamese orphans to new homes in the United States. Along with saving the orphans, the government concentrated on getting Americans and Vietnamese who were working for U.S. agencies out of the country.

When Saigon fell, tens of thousands of people could not wait any longer to leave Vietnam. About 130,000 Vietnamese fled over the coming weeks. The U.S. government helped about 65,000 of the refugees to leave by boat or by airplane. The other 65,000 made their own arrangements for leaving the country. When these refugees arrived in America, they stayed in refugee camps on military bases, set up through a program called Operation New Life.

The refugees who did not receive help directly from the United States fled to other Southeast Asian countries, such as Thailand, where there were American military bases for many of them. Eventually, most of these refugees ended up going through Operation New Life and arriving in the United States. Voluntary agencies (VOLAGs) worked to find sponsors for the refugees and to help them resettle in the United States. These organizations tried to distribute the refugees across the country, hoping they would enter into American society and not become isolated within their own ethnic communities.

Refugee Programs and Organizations

The American response to the arrival of nearly 130,000 Indochinese refugees was mixed. In 1975, the U.S. economy was weak. Many people felt that the arrival of the refugees would only make the economic situation worse, and that the U.S. government should concentrate on helping its own people. Others wanted to do all they could for the new arrivals. Special programs helped the refugees to learn English and to receive social and medical care. The VOLAGs placed the Vietnamese children in school and helped the adults to find work.

Most of the refugees ended up staying in the United States, although a few thousand went to other countries. In general, they did not have too many problems fitting in with American society. A lot of the people in this first wave of refugees came from middle-class backgrounds. More than a quarter of them had a college education. Within two years of their arrival, almost 95 percent of them had found jobs; within seven years, there was a higher employment rate among the first wave of Indochinese refugees than among the U.S. population in general.

In 1976, a year after the end of the Vietnam War, Canada accepted about 6,500 Vietnamese refugees. Vietnamese communities already existed in Canada before the 1970s, most of them in the French-Canadian province of Quebec because so many Vietnamese immigrants already spoke French as a result of France's occupation. Sixty-five percent of the first-wave refugees resettled in Quebec, where many relatives of the refugees had already settled.

By the end of 1975, the American camps for Indochinese refugees were closing down. Tens of thousands of refugees, many of whom had arrived from Cambodia and Laos (which also had an oppressive government), were in Thailand and still in need of assistance. The United States set up additional programs to bring them to America. This refugee group generally found it more difficult to assimilate into American society. Unlike the Vietnamese refugees, few of the Cambodians and the Laotians had much formal education. Many of the Vietnamese came from large cities where the influence of Western culture was strong, while the Cambodians and Laotians mostly came from small communities in the countryside.

Following the end of the Vietnam War, it seemed to many people that the Indochinese refugee crisis would soon come to an end. Lionel Rosenblatt of the Interagency Task Force, one of the U.S. government organizations that had helped with the refugee resettlement program, said: "[At the end of 1975], by and large we thought the evacuation would be it. There wasn't ever a vision that this would be an ongoing refugee program." In 1976, though, a huge second wave of refugees started leaving Indochina.

The Boat People

Because they disagreed with government policies in their countries, many Indochinese refugees had been denied basic rights, tortured, and placed in camps for "re-education." Their only option seemed to be flight. Thousands came by boat to other Southeast Asian countries, especially Thailand and Malaysia, but the authorities in these countries did not welcome them in. Refugee boats were stopped from landing and forced to go back to sea.

This new wave of Indochinese refugees became known as "boat people." The U.S. government created new refugee programs, allowing thousands to enter the country. But the crisis of the boat people grew steadily worse. In 1978, the totals of refugees fleeing by boat started to double—even triple—every month. Thousands drowned, and many were killed in pirate attacks at sea. Although the United States and other Western countries were trying to help as many refugees as possible, they could not keep up with the huge numbers of boat people leaving Indochina every day. Some people were brave and desperate enough to try sailing as far as the Australian coast. The U.S. government saw it was necessary to stop the refugees from fleeing in unsafe boats and embarking on dangerous journeys.

Americans began to fear that the U.S. government would repeat the mistakes it made during World War II, when it turned away many thousands of Jewish refugees whose lives were threatened. Canadians had similar feelings about the boat people. In November 1978, the Canadian government offered to accept 600 out of 2,500 Indochinese refugees on board a ship that had arrived in the Hong Kong harbor, but many Canadians also felt that they could have and should have done more.

In 1979, the United States established the Orderly Departure Program (ODP). The ODP allowed Vietnamese refugees to go directly to the United States from Vietnam. Through this program, the refugees could avoid the dangers of boat travel and receive help entering the United States. At first, the main purpose of the ODP was to help Vietnamese people to rejoin family members already in the United States. Later, others benefited from the program, including children born to American soldiers and Vietnamese women during and after the country's war.

In 1979 the number of boat people started to decline. Other UN countries, which had been reluctant before to assist the refugees, were more willing to help after observing the efforts of the United States and Canada. In 1980, the United States accepted 164,000 Indochinese refugees for resettlement. After 1981, the Indochinese refugee situation was no longer viewed as a crisis; however, the ODP has continued to operate because many people still flee from Indochina. Between 1988 and 2001, more than 343,000 Vietnamese refugees were resettled in the United States. There have been a number of congressional bills that required the State Department to continue processing and considering the cases of Vietnamese refugees—one such bill,

H.R. 1840, became law in May 2002. The legislation stemmed from a concern that individuals who were imprisoned by the communist government during the refugee crisis were not given the opportunity to apply for refugee status. There was also the concern that during the years of refugee processing, the Vietnamese interpreters used by the U.S. government may have encouraged refugees not to speak freely, or failed to pass along all relevant information to U.S. officials.

By the end of the 1980s, it was becoming more difficult for immigration officials to determine whether certain Indochinese arrivals were really qualified to claim refugee status. The 1989 Comprehensive Plan of Action for Indo-Chinese Refugees (CPA), developed at an international conference, reduced the number of Indochinese people claiming refugee status in North America. The CPA encouraged the Vietnamese not to leave on their own by boat, but to leave and resettle through official programs. If they wanted to return to their own country, they were helped to do so.

Vietnamese refugees on board a police boat, southwest of Hong Kong, 1989. More than two decades after the Vietnam War, hundreds of Indochinese people are still escaping repressive governments. Although it is not as active today as it was in the 1970s, the Orderly Departure Program still helps resettle these refugees in the United States.

Today, people who came from Indochina as refugees can be found all over the United States and Canada. They have had to cope with cultural differences, language barriers, and the general trauma of the refugee experience. In some cases, they have also had to overcome prejudice in their new communities.

In the United States, the largest numbers of Indochinese refugees are in California, Texas, and the state of Washington. In general, Vietnamese refugees have had the most success in adapting to American life. Cambodian and Laotian refugees have had greater problems with unemployment and poverty. Also, many of them have also struggled to learn English, a language very different from their own. Still, every Indochinese refugee has a different story. According to Walter Barnes, California's state refugee coordinator, "there are some tremendous successes and some tremendous failures. In the middle is a bunch of people trying to do their best."

The Indochinese in Canada

Between 1979 and 1981, Canada accepted around 50,000 Vietnamese refugees, as part of the country's first major refugee resettlement program under its new immigration laws. The program reflected a stronger commitment toward helping refugees. The government and private sponsors helped the refugees to resettle all over the country. Many family members who at some point had been separated during the move from Vietnam were reunited in Canada. Some parts of Canada made a special effort to resettle the refugees. In Ottawa, the capital of Canada, 4,000 Indochinese refugees were quickly resettled through Project 4000. During the 1980s and 1990s, Canada continued to resettle or give temporary refugee status to many Indochinese refugees. Between 1989 and 1995, the CPA helped nearly 23,000 Indochinese refugees to resettle in Canada.

Many Indochinese refugees live in the provinces of British Columbia, Alberta, Ontario, and Quebec. During the 1990s, about one-fifth of all the nearly 100,000 Vietnamese people in Canada lived in Montreal, the largest city in Quebec. A much smaller number of Cambodian and Laotian refugees have entered Canada.

These refugees in Canada have faced challenges similar to those in the United States, yet some may argue that Canada has perhaps been even more welcoming toward Indochinese culture. Surprisingly, there are more organizations committed to the preservation of Indochinese cultural identity in Canada, especially in Quebec, than there are in the United States.

The years of conflict in Vietnam and other parts of Indochina left behind a tragic legacy. Millions had to flee their homes, triggering the largest refugee crisis in history. Before the Indochinese refugee crisis, the United States and Canada never had to deal with a refugee movement on such a large scale. Eventually, both countries rose to the challenge. Through new laws, government programs, and the generosity of individuals and private organizations, more than a million Indochinese refugees were able to rebuild their lives in North America.

4 CRISIS IN THE CARIBBEAN

The large Caribbean island of Cuba lies less than 100 miles (161 kilometers) south of the tip of Florida. Just a short distance to the east of Cuba, across the Windward Passage, is Haiti. This country occupies the western side of another large island, Hispaniola, whose eastern side is occupied by the Dominican Republic.

For many people, the word *Caribbean* brings to mind beautiful beaches and a restful way of life. However, Cuba and Haiti have suffered from political repression and desperate economic problems for decades. Since 1959, many refugees have fled from Cuba to the United States. Haitian refugees have been leaving their country for the United States since the early 1970s. Differences in U.S. policy toward Cuban and Haitian refugees have caused controversy for years.

Cuban Refugee History

Before 1898, Cuba was a Spanish colony. Many Americans had long believed that Cuba would one day become a part of the United States. The U.S. helped Cuba to free itself from Spanish rule in 1898, after which it became officially independent. A longstanding agreement was then forged in which Cuba allowed the United States to intervene in its affairs. Over the next 60 years, thousands of Cubans came to the U.S., a majority of them settling in Florida. They became an important part of the American economy and culture.

◄ Cuban president Fidel Castro delivers a speech shortly after leading a coup to oust dictator Fulgencio Batista, January 1959. Castro instituted a communist regime as president, and many Cuban refugees who have since emerged have received asylum as a result of the anti-communist policies of the United States and Canada.

In 1959, a group of rebels led by Fidel Castro overthrew the dictator Fulgencio Batista, and Castro established his own communist government. Because of the U.S. government's anti-communist policy, the political ties between Cuba and the United States were completely broken by 1961. Immediately, a group of mostly upper-class Cubans left for the United States, hoping that Castro would soon be overthrown and that they could then return to a stabilized country. When it became clear that the Castro government was not a temporary one, an increasing number of Cubans started leaving for the United States. The U.S. government began arranging for daily flights from Cuba.

Once in the United States, Cuban refugees received assistance through the Nine-Point Program, which provided access to health and job services, schooling, and other essentials. This program fell under the Migration and Refugee Assistance Act of 1962. In Miami, Florida, the Cuban Refugee Emergency Center assisted with job placement and resettlement. Cubans called the center *El refugio*—"the Refuge" in Spanish.

Between 1960 and 1962, more than 150,000 people left Cuba through the airlift program. Because so many of these refugees were wealthy, they have been called the "Golden Exiles." The Cuban Missile Crisis of 1962 interrupted the airlift program for three years. In 1965, the program was resumed. The "freedom flights," which were stopped in 1973, brought nearly 250,000 Cubans to the United States. Over time, the Castro government tried to impede people from leaving by imposing heavier restrictions, such as allowing them to leave with only a very small amount of money. Eventually, that amount was reduced to nothing.

Still, many people continued to leave Cuba. Most of them moved to Florida, with large populations settling in Miami and the surrounding Dade County. Others went to New York, Los Angeles, and other parts of the United States where there were many Spanish speakers.

In the 1960s and 1970s, the attorney general had authority to

Refugees from Central America

Like so many other areas of the world, Central America has suffered from refugee crises. During the 1980s and 1990s, countries such as El Salvador, Guatemala, Honduras, and Nicaragua experienced civil war, human rights abuses, and extreme poverty. By 1990, it was estimated that there were 2 million Central American displaced people in the world. Many of these people are internally displaced; others have moved around to various Central American countries, Mexico, or the United States.

Despite the refugee crises in these countries, most Central American refugees have not entered the United States legally. There has been no "refugee processing" in the region (U.S. officials interviewing potential refugees in Central America.) Therefore, the primary option for Central Americans fleeing oppressive governments and violence in the 1970s and 1980s was to come to the United States and seek asylum. In 1985, a group of religious and human rights organizations collaborated on behalf of Guatemalan and Salvadoran asylum applicants and filed the *ABC v. Meese* lawsuit. The suit claimed that the U.S. government was unfairly dismissing legitimate claims of persecution, in part due to U.S. support for their governments. The lawsuit was finally settled in 1991 in favor of the asylum seekers. Those who were denied asylum before were at least offered another interview to reassess their claims.

However, when Congress passed the Illegal Immigration Reform and Immigrant Responsibility Act (IIRAIRA) in 1996, it became harder for individuals who lived in the country illegally to avoid deportation. Provisions of the act adversely affected many Central Americans. In 1997, after the Central American immigrant issue received much public attention, Congress passed the Nicaraguan and Central American Relief Act (NACARA). The law lowered the standard that Salvadorans and Guatemalans—including those in the *ABC* class-action lawsuit—had to meet in order to remain in the country. In addition, NACARA made it even easier for Nicaraguans to stay in the United States: generally speaking, it gave those who arrived in the country before 1995 permanent residence or green cards. Many observers believed that Nicaraguans received preferential treatment as a result of their greater political influence among Republicans in Congress.

At certain times, Canada has allowed groups of Central Americans to enter the country. In 1983, Salvadorans made up over 40 percent of all people moving to Canada from Central and South America. With the help of the Canadian government and some churches, 296 political prisoners and their families entered Canada in the early 1980s. In 1984, a special initiative allowed some Guatemalans to come to Canada as refugees.

Miami, Florida, has been the most popular place to resettle for Cuban refugees for over four decades. Throughout the 1960s the city's Cuban Refugee Emergency Center provided job placement and resettlement services to Cubans.

grant what was known as parole to people entering the United States. Parole gave Cubans permission to be in the country, yet it did not grant them permanent residence (the right to stay permanently). On the local level, communities that saw large-scale refugee resettlement made their own adjustments. For example, in Dade County schools instituted programs that helped refugee children learn English.

By the early 1970s, most of the Cuban arrivals in America were from low-income backgrounds. When the "freedom flights" ended, the number of Cuban arrivals dropped significantly. Over the next few years, many of the Cuban refugees coming to America first went to Spain. The U.S. government established programs that would bring these refugees over from Spain and reunite them with family members in the United States.

During the rest of the 1970s, the number of Cubans claiming refugee status in the United States decreased and remained at a manageable level. Relations between the Cuban exiles and Fidel Castro improved, and Castro began allowing Cuban exiles to visit their homeland. He also allowed for the release of 3,000 political prisoners. In 1980, no one was prepared for the events that would make the Cuban refugee crisis known to all Americans.

The Mariel Boatlift

In April 1980, 3,500 Cubans asked for asylum at the Embassy of Peru in Cuba, stating that they disagreed strongly with the policies of Castro's government. Peru did not want to take them as political refugees, however, and so the United States agreed to accept them. Fidel Castro announced that he was lifting the restrictions on those who wanted to leave Cuba, but on the condition that the refugees go directly to the United States and no other country.

On April 21, thousands of Cubans living in Florida arrived in Cuba's Mariel Harbor in hired boats. They were the first wave of Cuban immigrants and Cuban Americans to bring their friends and relatives to Florida. Under U.S. immigration law, the Mariel boatlift was illegal, yet the government made an exception in the interest of helping these particular refugees

A boat full of Cuban refugees arrives in Key West, Florida, as part of the massive Mariel boatlift of 1980. More than 125,000 refugees were involved in the boatlift, which was prompted by President Castro's sudden decision to lift restrictions on emigration.

escape. President Jimmy Carter announced that the United States would welcome the refugees with "an open heart and open arms." Over the course of seven months, 125,000 Cubans had arrived by boat.

The Mariel boatlift operation became difficult to manage because the refugee group was not limited to friends and relatives of those already living in the United States. Following Castro's directive to get rid of Cuba's "antisocial elements." Cuban officials had opened a number of the country's jails and mental hospitals and put the inmates onto the Mariel boats. A U.S. House Appropriations Committee report found that approximately 10 percent of the Mariel Cubans may have possessed a mental illness or criminal background that would have made them ineligible to enter the United States under the law.

The American public was less supportive of this new wave of refugees than it had been of past arrivals on the shores of Florida. The U.S. economy at the time was weak, and many people felt that the sudden arrival of thousands of refugees would only make matters worse. Around the end of May, the government began to seize boats and impose fines. The Mariel boatlift came to an end.

Most of the Mariel refugees, who became known as "Marielitos," were able to stay in the United States, though in some cases their status of refugees remained uncertain for years. Some criminals were classified as "excludable aliens"—in the past, a term used to describe those who had not yet entered the country. The refugees who were criminals and had already entered the United States were detained indefinitely, although they had already served time for their crimes. Others were classified as "entrants, status pending."

The Marielitos faced unique challenges, some of which were posed by Cubans already resettled in America. Marielitos and the pre-Mariel refugees disagreed over many things. Siro del Castillo, former director of a refugee center in Miami, understood the source of the conflict: "The Marielitos demanded respect for having to endure the Castro regime. Meanwhile, the exiles [pre-Mariel refugees] were saying, 'We worked very hard to get what we have.'"

However, the Marielitos believed they had also endured much to become a part of American society, and they were ready to take advantage of their new opportunities. By 1985, most of them were able to become permanent residents. A few years later, they were able to start bringing family members over from Cuba. Like earlier generations of refugees, the Marielitos were eager to help new refugees from Cuba, even if they were not family members. During the 1980s, they had great success in assimilating into American society, enjoying the highest levels of employment of any immigrant group in Florida.

Cuban refugees continued to enter the United States with little difficulty until 1994, when the U.S. government had to confront major refugee crises involving thousands of Cubans and Haitians wishing to enter the country. These two crises were related in many ways, and so it is helpful to first become familiar with Haitian refugee history leading up to 1994.

The Haitian Refugees

For decades, oppressive government policies have motivated many Haitians to flee the country. People today blame these policies and their negative effects on a family of dictators—Francois Duvalier (Papa Doc), who ruled from 1957 to 1971, and his son Jean-Claude Duvalier (Baby Doc), who ruled from 1971 to 1986. Papa Doc and Baby Doc called themselves "presidents for life," meaning that they prohibited presidential elections to take place while they were in power. During the reign of the Duvaliers, many Haitians were persecuted for their political views and denied basic human rights. They also suffered under very poor economic conditions: about 90 percent of Haitians lived well below the poverty level.

Before 1970, a small number of Haitians, primarily consisting of political refugees, had come to live in the United States. But it was not until the early 1970s that Haitians began arriving to the United States in large groups. They usually set out for

President François "Papa Doc" Duvalier (1907–71) initiated a legacy of government repression in Haiti that was preserved by his son, Jean-Claude "Baby Doc," the country's president from 1971 to 1986. Although many Haitians during the dictatorship years were victims of persecution, only a fraction of those applying as refugees were accepted by the United States.

Florida, traveling by boat across the same stretch of water as those Cuban refugees bound for the United States.

But the similarities between the plight of Cuban and Haitian refugees end there, because since 1981 the U.S. Coast Guard has regularly stopped Haitian boats and forced them to turn back. They have even towed some boats back out to sea to ensure that the Haitians do not attempt entry again. Most of the Haitians who have managed to reach Florida have been denied asylum, forcing them to be deported or to join the Haitian community as undocumented immigrants.

One crucial piece of legislation, the Cuban Adjustment Act, is a primary factor behind why Haitian and Cuban refugees have been treated differently by the various U.S. immigration bureaus. Passed in 1966, the law allows Cubans, regardless of how they arrived to the United States, to become permanent residents (green card holders) after being physically present in the country for one year or more. Between 1966 and 1998, approximately 618,000 Cubans adjusted to permanent residence, according to the Congressional Research Service.

The Cuban Adjustment Act also explains why from 1966 until the present day, Cubans have generally not been detained for long periods of time after arriving in the United States.

Because Cubans are eligible to become permanent residents after being a year in the country, it makes little sense to spend taxpayer dollars on keeping individuals detained for a year who will simply be released after that period.

The Cuban Adjustment Act was a result of the U.S. opposition to Cuba's communist government, an opposition that remains strong to this day. In contrast, the United States enjoyed friendly relations with Haiti's government for many years, which subsequently disrupted the plans of Haitian refugees. Although many people in Haiti have been persecuted, U.S. immigration officials have typically viewed Haitian refugees as individuals escaping poverty, not political oppression. Critics of U.S. policy say that Haitians leave their country for all kinds of reasons other than economic hardship.

Since no law like the Cuban Adjustment Act exists for Haitians—or any other nationality—those who land in the United States from Haiti must demonstrate that they have a "well-founded fear of persecution." Economic deprivation, a generalized fear of violence, or dissatisfaction with the political regime is not sufficient under U.S. law to receive asylum.

The number of Haitian boat people coming to the United States increased in 1980, around the time of the Mariel boatlift. Human rights groups and others demanded that the Cubans and the Haitians be treated in the same way. Like many of the Cuban refugees, the Haitians were classified as "entrants, status pending," but unlike the Cubans, they still could not apply to stay permanently in the United States.

In 1981, the U.S. government made an agreement directly with the Haitian government. Haiti would take back people who were trying to leave and enter the United States illegally, and the U.S. Coast Guard would start to interdict, or stop from entering the country, all boats arriving from Haiti. Although the Coast Guard was only supposed to send back undocumented immigrants, not refugees, most Haitians attempting entry were turned back between 1981 and 1991.

In 1986, Jean-Bertrand Aristide began a tumultuous term as elected president, as Haiti made initial attempts at democracy. For a time, the country's situation improved under his rule, and fewer people tried to leave. In 1991, a coup overthrew Aristide. Political persecution and other problems increased once again. Soon another wave of Haitians tried to leave the country. Some went across the eastern border to the Dominican Republic, while others headed for the United States.

Although U.S. officials continued to interdict Haitians who were on their way to the United States, they temporarily stopped returning them to Haiti in 1991 and instead moved them to the military base at Guantánamo Bay, Cuba. There they went through a screening process to determine if they could apply for refugee status in the United States. Out of 34,000 Haitians taken

A group of Haitian refugees is picked up by the U.S. Coast Guard in November 1991. A new wave of refugees emerged that year after the overthrow of President Jean-Bertrand Aristide paved the way for another period of persecution and oppression.

to Guantánamo Bay during this period, 10,500 were able to go to the United States and apply for refugee status, although most of them were not admitted. Guantánamo Bay was called a "safe haven," but some human rights organizations argued that it was more like a prison than a place of shelter.

After six months, Guantánamo Bay was closed to the Haitians. Once again, the Coast Guard began sending refugee boats back, and the repatriation program continued until 1994, the year that the overwhelming numbers of Haitians and Cubans attempting to emigrate led to major refugee crises.

The Refugee Crises of 1994

Cuba began to experience serious economic problems in the early 1990s. The 1991 collapse of the Soviet Union, Cuba's communist ally, made matters worse for the country. An increasing number of Cubans tried to leave the country and go to the United States. In 1994, the situation became desperate. When Cuban officials tried to stop the refugees from leaving, they staged riots in protest. Even worse, some refugees hijacked ferries in an attempt to reach Florida. The Cuban government once again lifted restrictions on leaving the country, and much like the Mariel boatlift of 1980, Cubans started departing in large numbers. The U.S. Coast Guard picked up many of the 30,000 who fled, though dozens died at sea.

The U.S. government believed that it could not deal with such large numbers of people claiming refugee status. Most of the refugees were taken to Guantánamo Bay instead of Florida. In August 1994, President Bill Clinton's administration reached an agreement with the Cuban government. The U.S. would no longer allow all Cuban refugees to enter the country, and the Cuban authorities would try to restrict the mass departure of its citizens. The U.S. would hand out, at minimum, 20,000 entry permits every year, though these were only for those who were granted permission to emigrate by Castro's regime. The U.S. government began holding lotteries every few years to determine who would receive the 20,000 slots.

Haitian refugees saw their situation improve temporarily in 1994. In June, the U.S. government set up a refugee application center on board the USNS *Comfort*, a hospital ship. The U.S. Navy stationed the *Comfort* off the coast of Jamaica. Coast Guard officers took interdicted Haitian refugees on board the ship and processed their applications. Many of the Haitian refugees who went on board were granted refugee status.

Over the next few weeks, though, the *Comfort* could not cope with the waves of refugees fleeing Haiti. The United States responded by opening additional refugee application centers. Haitian soldiers destroyed boats in an attempt to stop people from leaving. During one incident at Baie du Mesle, on the southern coast of Haiti, soldiers fired on a boat carrying hundreds of refugees. When the panicked refugees tried to dodge the gunfire, dozens of them fell into the water and drowned.

And yet the flow of refugees continued to increase. President Aristide, in exile while waiting to return to power, refused to urge Haitians against leaving. "It would be immoral to ask people whose very lives are at risk to stay in Haiti, a Haiti I am compelled to describe as a house on fire," he said.

Although the United States could not process such a large number of refugees, American officials also realized that they could not send the Haitians back to their country at this time. Once again, Guantánamo Bay was opened to the Haitians. From July until September 1994, 21,000 Haitians stayed at the naval base. In September, after the U.S. military threatened to invade Haiti if the regime did not relinquish its control, an accord was reached. When Aristide returned to power, most of the Haitians at Guantánamo Bay returned as well.

In the beginning of 1995, thousands of Cubans were still being held at Guantánamo Bay. In May, the U.S. government agreed to allow most of them to enter the country. But the era of easy migration for Cuban refugees was coming to an end. Over the next year, the United States and Cuba agreed that Cubans who wanted to enter the United States would have to go through legal programs for refugees and immigrants.

The United States developed the "wet foot, dry foot" policy toward Cuban refugees. Simply put, those Cubans who made it to shore would be allowed to stay and those Cubans who were interdicted at sea and never made it to U.S. soil would be returned to Cuba after getting an opportunity to apply for refugee status.

In 1998, the U.S. Congress passed the Haitian Refugee Immigration Fairness Act. Under this new law, Haitians who had applied for asylum before 1996 were now able to apply for permanent residence. Since 1994 the number of Haitian refugees trying to come to the United States has been relatively low. Most refugees are picked up by the U.S. Coast Guard and denied entry. Another attempted journey in October 2002 sparked controversy once again. A ship of more than 200 Haitian refugees ran aground off Key Biscayne, Miami, and as usual, the refugees were picked up and detained. Around the same time, eight Cuban refugees who arrived at the Key West airport were allowed to join their relatives in Florida.

The U.S. naval base at Guantánamo Bay, Cuba, has often served as a holding center for Cuban and Haitian refugees during major crises. In the late 1990s the base also housed thousands of Kosovar refugees escaping the war in the former Yugoslavia.

In a controversial policy decision first implemented in December 2001, the Bush administration started to detain almost all Haitians who made it to U.S. soil via boat. Attorney General John Ashcroft stated that the policy was necessary to prevent a mass migration and, in the spring of 2003, invoked national security to justify the continuing detention of the Haitians. This policy meant that rather than being let out on bond while their asylum claims were being decided, Haitian men and women would remain locked up for nine months or more in prison, albeit separated from criminals.

Refugee Life in the United States

Today, a large number of Cubans and Haitians live in New York City. There are also Cuban communities in New Jersey and California. But Florida has by far the highest Cuban and Haitian populations in the United States, and in fact is home for two-thirds of the 1.2 million Cubans living in the country.

The population of Miami is 30 percent Cuban. The city's Little Havana neighborhood is a popular area for tourists, featuring Cuban restaurants, stores, and monuments dedicated to Cuban figures of the past and present. The headquarters of Alpha 66, a Cuban anti-Castro political group, is in Little Havana's Plaza de la Cubanidad. Little Haiti, though much less wealthy than Little Havana, also has colorful stores, especially those that sell Caribbean food and religious items.

Many Cubans are involved in U.S. politics, and have a clear influence on American policy regarding their home country. Cubans living in the United States come from a wide variety of social and educational backgrounds. Those who arrived before the Mariel boatlift were generally well educated. They have contributed greatly to helping the refugees who came during and after the Mariel boatlift.

Some Cubans are well established in the United States and would prefer not to leave under any circumstances. Others would choose to leave if Castro's communist government came to an end. Alex Cambert, a correspondent for the morning TV

A Cuban American enjoys an espresso outside a Cuban café in Little Havana, Miami. The state of Florida is home to the largest population of Cubans, and two-thirds of the 1.2 million Cubans living in the United States take residence in Miami.

program *Good Morning America*, gave an account of his family's immigrant history. He said:

> My father came from Cuba for what he thought was a temporary stay, and is still hoping for the demise of Castro. I'm born here and know that my parents' struggle gave me the freedom to choose, even if that means rejecting the very things my parents adhere to.

The Haitian community in the United States has experienced more serious problems than the Cuban community has. In 1996, it was estimated that there were 105,000 undocumented Haitians living in the U.S.

Haitian immigrants have worked hard to become a productive part of American society. Some outspoken migrants have drawn attention to the differences in how the government has treated Cuban and Haitian refugees. All have faced the challenge of becoming American while still remaining Haitian.

5 REFUGEES FROM THE MIDDLE EAST

The Middle East lies at one of the world's major crossroads. It shares regional borders with Asia, contains a number of North African countries, and according to some definitions, includes Turkey, a country with strong European connections. Other major countries of the Middle East are Iran, Iraq, Israel, and Saudi Arabia.

Many people imagine this vast region as uninhabitable with dry, burning deserts, yet actually it has been the site of some of the world's oldest and more advanced civilizations. Although the Muslim religion is dominant in the Middle East, the region is also the birthplace of the Jewish and Christian religions. The Western world has always been interested in the Middle East; since the early 20th century, it has taken particular interest in its oil and other valuable natural resources.

For hundreds of years, the mixture of the Middle East's different religions, political systems, and cultures, accompanied by the intervention of outside countries, have generated continual turmoil. Countries have been racked by war and religious persecution. Especially since the 1950s, the eyes of the world have turned again and again to this troubled region, where wars and oppressive governments have created millions of refugees. Afghanistan, Lebanon, Iraq, Israel, Iran, and other Middle Eastern countries all have major refugee movements in their national histories.

◀ Iranian demonstrators march with a shrouded body in 1978; mourning ceremonies like this one were often accompanied by rioting and violence between Islamic rebels and the Iranian government. The Iranian Revolution ended with the ascension of the Ayatollah Khomeini in January 1979, who instituted an oppressive regime that produced hundreds of thousands of refugees.

The Iranian Refugee Crisis

Until 1935, Iran was called Persia. For centuries, it was part of the much larger Persian Empire. In the early years of the 20th century, Persia was one of the first Middle Eastern countries in which oil reserves were found. The discovery sparked the interest of many Western countries, which began to influence the region's politics and culture. In 1908, the Anglo-Persian Oil Company was established and soon became one of the most important oil companies in the world.

The shah, or king, made several changes to Persia, including changing its name to Iran in 1935. He also reorganized Iran's legal and educational systems to be more like those of Europe, and even insisted that Iranians wear European-style clothing. After 1953, when the government of the powerful anti-Western politician Mohammed Mossadegh was overthrown, Iran gradually became even more Westernized. Other Middle Eastern countries began to view Iran as a threat, arguing that its Western-influenced ambitions went against the principles of Islam. The stage was set for what became known as the Islamic Revolution (1978–79).

In the early 1960s, a group of Muslim clerics opposed many of the current shah's liberal reforms. Their leader, the Ayatollah Khomeini, was sent into exile in Iraq. By 1978, many Iranians

Under the Ayatollah Ruhollah Khomeini (1900–1989), Iranians were subject to the worst forms of persecution. Many of his political opponents were executed before they could flee the country.

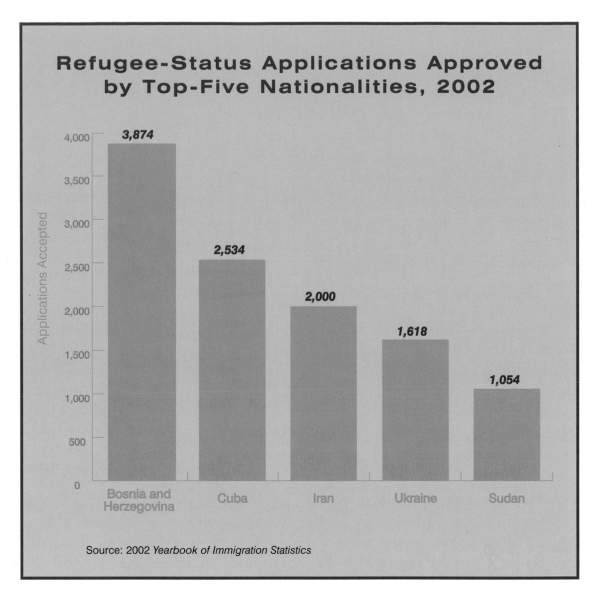

Refugee-Status Applications Approved by Top-Five Nationalities, 2002

Applications Accepted

- Bosnia and Herzegovina: 3,874
- Cuba: 2,534
- Iran: 2,000
- Ukraine: 1,618
- Sudan: 1,054

Source: 2002 *Yearbook of Immigration Statistics*

were unhappy with the shah's government, particularly its shifts toward Westernization and its heavy spending. Khomeini, who was living in Paris, insisted that the shah step down. In January 1979, the shah left Iran, and Khomeini returned to take control.

Before the Islamic Revolution, many Iranians had left their country to study or to work in other countries. Most of them had planned to come back to Iran, though they were impeded by Khomeini's new intolerant regime. Khomeini declared that the other Middle Eastern countries were not truly Muslim, and that the Islamic Revolution should be extended to overthrow these countries' governments. Under the shah, Iran had been an ally of the United States. Now, Khomeini viewed the United States as the greatest enemy of Islam.

The Iranian hostage crisis, in which 52 Americans were held in captivity between November 1979 and January 1981, made relations between Iran and the United States even worse. Supporters of the shah and of other political parties who feared persecution under Khomeini's regime decided to flee Iran as refugees. Some of them were executed before they could leave the country.

People who belonged to religions other than Islam also became targets. They included Jews and members of the Baha'i religion, considered an Islamic heresy by the state. At the time of the Islamic Revolution, there were more than 300,000 Baha'is in Iran. Under the new regime, Baha'is had their property and jobs taken away; some lost their lives. Realizing that the group was facing a desperate situation, UNHCR announced that any Iranian Baha'i could claim refugee status. The Baha'is, along with other religious minorities, became one of the largest refugee groups to flee Iran.

Hundreds of thousands of Iranians left Iran after the revolution. Many of them remained in Turkey or Pakistan. By 1988, there may have been close to 2 million Iranian refugees in these countries. In the 1980s, the situation was made worse by the war between Iran and Iraq, which lasted from 1980 to 1988. In Western countries, it took a long time for awareness of the Iranian refugee problem to develop.

Many of the Iranians who fled joined family members who already lived in the United States and Canada. They hoped to return to Iran at a later date, so some only requested asylum after they had been in North America for a number of years and realized that returning to Iran meant risking their lives and freedom. The Ayatollah Khomeini died in 1989, but another supreme leader, Ali Khamenei, replaced him. Khamenei's great influence over Iran's elected president has kept the government

Vancouver, British Columbia, is home to one of Canada's largest Iranian communities. A diverse group of nearly 30,000 Iranians claim residence in the city.

repressive, especially toward political and religious minorities. Refugees continued to leave Iran in the 1990s and the first decade of the 21st century.

Life for the Iranian Refugee

Canada and the United States have welcomed many Iranians. In 1982, Canada announced that it was creating a special program for Iranian refugees. Canada helped let in about 500 Iranian refugees that year, and another 500 in 1983. The refugee program concentrated on assisting Baha'is, and members of the religion raised money to help the refugees come and get settled in their new country. Canada continued to accept members of this group in the 1990s. Between 1990 and 1995, about 30,000 Iranians were granted asylum in North America, and 80 percent of them were accepted by Canada.

Between 1980 and 1989, more than 136,000 Iranians came

to the United States. Only some of these people fell into the category of "refugee"—on average, perhaps 4,000 every year. In a 1988 survey of Iranians in Los Angeles, about 40 percent of the people surveyed fit the definition of refugees. However, the researchers also said that only 27 percent had left for political or religious reasons, making them "pure refugees." From 1990 to 1998, less than 113,000 Iranians came to the United States, and again, only some of them were classified as refugees. Between 1981 and 2001, less than 60,000 Iranians entered the country classified as refugees. Since the mid-1990s, the number of Iranian arrivals in North America has gone down, as it has in other parts of the world.

In the United States today, the largest Iranian communities are in Los Angeles, San Francisco, New York, and Washington, D.C. Southern California has the highest Iranian population in the world outside of Iran itself. Some estimates say that there are as many as 600,000 Iranians in this area. Iranians in Los Angeles like to call the city "Tehrangeles" after Tehran, Iran's capital city. The average Iranian in the United States earns more money and has more education than the average American. Many Iranians have had a lot of success in the business world. One famous example is Iranian businessman Pierre Omidyar, who founded eBay, the Internet auction company.

The American-Iranian community is interested in preserving its cultural identity. In the United States, there are many Iranian newspapers and magazines, radio stations, and cultural organizations. In California alone, there are almost 40 of these

The Iranian Hostage Crisis

The Iranian hostage crisis began on November 4, 1979. On that day, about 500 Iranian students, angry that the exiled shah had been allowed into the United States for medical treatment, seized the U.S. embassy in Tehran. Negotiations and a rescue mission to free the hostages failed. On January 20, 1981, the hostages were finally freed. The crisis had lasted for 444 days.

special organizations. Along with maintaining their cultural pride, Iranians have also pursued an American identity. Sanam Ansari, the president of the Iranian Students Group at the University of California, says: "They have a word in Persian, 'do-hava.' It means 'two-weathered.' You're not completely American and not completely Iranian." At the same time, Iranians have had to face prejudice. Ever since the Iranian hostage crisis, some Americans have associated Iran with terrorism and anti-Americanism; however, since Iranian refugees are typically not Muslim, this problem has affected them less than it has the general Iranian immigrant community.

Canada has large Iranian communities in several cities, including Montreal and Vancouver. In Vancouver, there are nearly 30,000 Iranians from different religious backgrounds, including the Muslim, Baha'i, Jewish, Zoroastrian, and Christian faiths. The Persian newspaper *Shahrvand-e-Vancouver* (in Persian, "Citizens of Vancouver") has a weekly circulation of 20,000 around Canada. Vancouver is a city whose residents have come from all over the world, and for many different reasons. Some Iranians say that the beautiful scenery surrounding Vancouver has drawn them to the city, especially the mountains of North Vancouver, which remind them of the mountains of Tehran.

Other Arab Refugees

Iranian refugees and immigrants are far from being the only Middle Eastern people to have come in large numbers to North America. Particularly in the United States, there are communities that have welcomed people from different Middle Eastern countries for over a century. One of these communities is Detroit, Michigan, and its surrounding suburbs, especially Dearborn. In the beginning of the 20th century, these communities became centers for Henry Ford's car production company.

Middle Eastern immigrants have been arriving in the United States since the 1870s. Many Middle Eastern laborers—a majority of them Lebanese men—found employment with Ford and other companies during the car manufacturing boom. Despite the low wages and dangerous nature of the work, the Ford Company still helped Michigan's Middle Eastern community to become established long before the end of World War II.

In the past 60 years, the Middle East has suffered through just as many wars and other crises as it has in past centuries. In 1948, Jewish leaders accepted a United Nations resolution to divide the region of Palestine, giving the Jewish people their own land. When the state of Israel was created, surrounding Arab nations launched an attack. Eventually, Israel took control of a great portion of Palestine. Millions of Palestinian Arabs became refugees, and some of them are still in refugee camps today, though many have settled in other parts of the world.

As a community that already had a large Arab population, Dearborn was a natural choice for Palestinian and other Arab

A Refugee Hero Finds a New Home

In 2003, humanitarian agencies and U.S. officials provided assistance to Iraqis who became refugees because of the Second Gulf War, fought between a U.S.–led coalition and Iraq in March and April of that year. Through one famous act of heroism during the war, one of those refugees secured the opportunity to resettle in the United States.

Mohammed al-Rehaief, a lawyer living in Iraq, approached U.S. soldiers in late March, informing them that he had spoken with an American prisoner of war in a hospital in Nasiriyah city. Risking his own life as an informant, al-Rahaief gave U.S. officers the details they needed to rescue Jessica Lynch, an Army supply clerk, on April 1.

As a show of gratitude for his invaluable assistance, the Department of Homeland Security offered Mohammed al-Rehaief, his wife, and their five-year-old daughter the option to resettle in the United States. After a short stay in a refugee camp, al-Rehaief departed for the United States with his family. They were granted "humanitarian parole," a form of refugee status typically reserved for those in need of medical treatment not available in their home country. In a public address, Homeland Security Secretary Tom Ridge said: "Mr. Al Rehaief should know Americans are grateful for his bravery and for his compassion."

refugees coming to the United States. In 1978 and 1982, Israeli invasions of Lebanon created many more refugees, some of whom went to the United States. In 1991, refugees fled from the Gulf War between Iraq and a coalition of Western and Middle Eastern countries. Since the Gulf War, over 3,000 Iraqi refugees have entered the United States through the Detroit area every year.

Today, there may be as many as 300,000 Arab Americans living in the Detroit area, and about 30,000 of them living in Dearborn. Many are Muslims, but there is also a sizable group of Christians. The Chaldeans, a group of Iraqi Christians, have left Iraq in large numbers. Refugees and immigrants of different Middle Eastern countries and faiths tend to group themselves according to their national origins. For instance, the main Yemeni community is on the south side of Dearborn. There are large Iraqi communities on the east and west sides of Detroit. Hoda Amine, who lives in Dearborn, called the community "a third culture . . . a microcosm of the Middle East in America's Midwest."

Although Middle Eastern groups generally prefer to live with people of the same background, many have tried to leave behind the disagreements that have caused so many problems in their home countries. Because of the fear of terrorism that has arisen after the September 2001 attacks, many Arab Americans feel that new anti-terrorism laws are targeting them and diminishing their rights. Sometimes Arab Americans have had to face discrimination and prejudice—problems that might have forced them to leave their home countries in the first place. Still, the Middle Eastern inhabitants of this region of Michigan are accustomed to working hard to maintain their Middle Eastern identity while still becoming American. Their success bodes well for future immigrants arriving to the area.

6 REFUGEES FROM EUROPE

Europe has seen millions of people become refugees and displaced persons within its borders, a significant portion of them a result of the two world wars. In the decades since the end of World War II, there have been other refugee movements within Europe, most starting in Russia and Eastern Europe. People have been forced to leave their countries because of the violent rise and fall of governments, political and religious persecution, or fighting between ethnic groups.

In the 1990s, crises in the former republic of Yugoslavia and the surrounding areas quickly created some of the largest refugee movements in history. In many cases, the people displaced by these conflicts have fled to other countries in Europe. The United States and Canada have also played important roles in helping these refugees by moving them to safer places and resettling them temporarily or permanently.

Hungarian Refugees

In the 1950s, the Soviet Union maintained control over the countries of Eastern Europe. There was very little political and religious freedom under the communist governments of these countries. Freedom of information was also limited. It was illegal to own or produce books and other publications that indicated or supported an anti-communist perspective. In Hungary, revolutionaries overthrew the Soviet-backed government in

◀An ethnic Albanian mother and child receive food handouts after they were left homeless by fighting, June 1999. Beginning in February 1998, the Kosovo crisis displaced 900,000 people. Member countries of the North Atlantic Treaty Organization (NATO), which includes the United States and Canada, agreed to take these refugees in, as they had done a few years before with victims of the war in Bosnia and Herzegovina.

October 1956 and attempted to set up their own government in its place. The revolution lasted for only a week. On November 4, the Soviet army entered the Hungarian capital and crushed the uprising.

Over the next few months, hundreds of thousands of Hungarians fled the country. Many of them went to Austria and other European countries. Partly because of their anti-communist policies, the United States and Canada also welcomed many of the Hungarian refugees. During the crisis, the United States accepted over 38,000 of the refugees, and for the first time, the government gave cash assistance to voluntary agencies to help these refugees resettle. Most of them were resettled in New York, New Jersey, Pennsylvania, and Ohio, where there were already many Hungarian immigrants.

There was some concern that a few of the Hungarian refugees might be communist spies, but the U.S. government still set aside rigid quota restrictions so that the refugees could enter the country in large numbers. A report by Vice President Richard Nixon to President Dwight Eisenhower said of the Hungarian refugees: "The large majority are young people—students, technicians, craftsmen and professional people." People with these skills were viewed as valuable additions to the United States. Nixon's report also stated:

> For the most part they were in the forefront of the fight for freedom. . . . The majority of the refugees who have been interviewed say that they left Hungary because of fear of liquidation or of deportation. The number of [communist] floaters and of those who left Hungary purely for economic reasons is relatively small.

The Canadian government accepted over 37,000 refugees resulting from the Hungarian crisis. A greater percentage of the Hungarian refugee population went to Canada than to the United States or any other country. As in the United States, there had been fears among Canadians that Soviet spies would enter the country with the refugees. Nonetheless, during the crisis the Canadian government changed its policy of accepting limited numbers of refugees from Soviet governments. J. W.

In a camp in Traiskirchen, Austria, Hungarian refugees receive food, November 1956. Soviet forces stormed Budapest, the Hungarian capital, to crush a popular uprising. In response, hundreds of thousands of Hungarians fled the country; some were welcomed by anti-communist countries like the United States and Canada.

Pickersgill, Minister of Immigration at the time, set up a Hungarian Immigration Branch and advised the Canadian officials dealing with the refugees: "Unless your Security Officer has serious reason to believe the applicant is a security risk, we would expect him to issue a security clearance."

Some of those fleeing the communist states were Jews, an ethnic group that had not been heartily accepted by Canada in the past. With the Hungarian crisis, though, Canadians started to overcome their prejudices against Jewish refugees. The Canadian federal government was mainly responsible for resettling the refugees, providing them with education, and helping them to find work. But the refugees also received help from voluntary organizations, universities, provincial governments, and private sponsors. As in the United States, most of the Hungarian refugees stayed permanently in Canada.

In 1968, Czechoslovakia faced a similar situation to that of Hungary in 1956. The "Prague Spring" revolution tried to

establish a more liberal socialist government in the place of the very restrictive regime that ruled the country. Once again, Soviet troops quickly stopped the revolution. Compared to the departure of refugees after the Hungarian revolution, much fewer refugees left the country after the Prague Spring. Canada accepted about 12,000 of the Czechoslovakian refugees. Their communist background was no longer considered much of a problem. Instead, the Canadian government looked at the refugees as valuable additions to the workforce, since most of them were young, well educated, and had the skills that employers needed. The refugees settled in different parts of Canada, with large clusters in provinces such as Ontario, Alberta, and British Columbia.

Throughout the 1980s and the 1990s, there were many Jewish refugees headed to North America from Russia, in addition to the large numbers of refugees coming from Indochina, the Caribbean, and the Middle East. In Russia, the Jews had faced discrimination and persecution for their background as well for as for their political and religious views. Israel was the traditional destination for this group, but many, especially those who were younger and less devoted to the Jewish faith, chose to move to the United States instead. In 1979, a peak year for departures, over 51,000 Jews left the Soviet Union. Almost two-thirds of them went to the United States.

The dispute over the free emigration of Soviet Jews became a major part of U.S.–Soviet summits and the overall topic of dialogue between the two countries. After the United States protested the Soviet invasion of Afghanistan in 1979, and even provided aid to Afghan rebels, one of the Soviet's government responses was to severely restrict the number of Jews permitted to leave the country each year. The thaw in U.S.–Soviet relations after Mikhail Gorbachev became Soviet leader in 1985 eventually helped restart the the next wave of emigrating Soviet Jews.

It was common for some Russian Jews to leave the Soviet Union with entry papers for Israel, but to change destinations along the way and go to the United States. The Israeli government feared that if the United States continued to accept Russian Jewish refugees who migrated in this manner, the Soviet government might start preventing them from emigrating. During the late 1980s and early 1990s, Russian Jews continued to leave the former Soviet Union. Many of them were still choosing the United States as their final destination, but by this time, the process was better regulated, and they could apply directly to the U.S. government for entry. In the 1990s, an increasing number of evangelical Christians also became refugees based on their fear of religious persecution in the former Soviet Union. Between 1988 and 2001, more than 460,000 refugees from the former Soviet Union came to the United States.

Refugees of the Balkans

During that same period, some of the worst refugee crises in world history arose in Eastern Europe. These crises came about because of changing situations and fighting within and around the Balkan states.

The area of Europe known as the Balkans lies to the east of Italy and the north of Greece. For hundreds of years, this region has been the scene of conflicts and shifting borders. In the Balkans, people from many different ethnic and religious backgrounds are situated together in a relatively small area. During the 1990s, the status of different areas within the Balkans had changed quickly and sometimes without much warning. Different ethnic groups turned on each other, and one of the results of those conflicts was a series of refugee crises.

In Kosovo, a southern province of the region of Serbia, the population was mainly made up of ethnic Albanians. The ethnic Albanians were the descendants of people from Albania, located just north of Greece, who had traveled farther north into Serbia. The province of Kosovo was very important to the Serbs because it had been the site of a major battle between Serbs and the Turks in 1389. Six hundred years later, in 1989, the Serbian leader Slobodan Milosevic took action against the ethnic Albanians in Kosovo. Serbs took over the provincial government and stole the jobs of ethnic Albanians. Thousands of Kosovar Albanians, especially young men, fled the region. Some went to Western Europe, while others went to the United States and Canada.

In 1991, the Socialist Federal Republic of Yugoslavia broke up when three of its regions, Slovenia, Croatia, and the Former Yugoslav Republic of Macedonia, declared independence. Between 1991 and 1995, millions of people became refugees or were internally displaced by the fighting, especially in the regions of Bosnia and Herzegovina. The atrocities of ethnic cleansing became known to the whole world, as ethnic groups tried to wipe out others within the regions.

The United Nations sent UNHCR relief operations and other representatives into the Balkans. Although UNHCR tried to help the victims of violence, it could do little to stop the ethnic cleansing and fighting. From 1992 to 1996, UNHCR organized an ongoing airlift into the Balkans. Airplanes brought food, medicine, and supplies to Sarajevo, the capital of Bosnia, which was the scene of some of the worst fighting. Many of the airplanes came from the United States and Canada.

Former Yugoslav president Slobodan Milosevic oversaw the attack on ethnic Albanians in Kosovo. In 1999 Milosevic was indicted as a war criminal for his role in ethnic cleansing in Yugoslavia.

During the Yugoslav war of the early 1990s, thousands of refugees were resettled in the United States and Canada. The United States took 38,000 refugees from Bosnia and Herzegovina during and after the war years. Canada took the same number of refugees from Bosnia and Herzegovina and other countries in the region. About 30 percent of these refugees were children, many of whom continued to suffer from the memories of what they had seen and experienced. In one U.S. school, young Bosnian refugees were asked to draw pictures of home. One student drew a picture of himself standing in front of men with guns, over which he wrote in his native Serbo-Croatian: "I was dreaming how they shot me." Despite their hardships, many Bosnians found that they could adjust to their new countries and to make a fresh start with their families.

In the United States, Chicago and St. Louis have the largest Bosnian populations. Before 1993, St. Louis did not have a large population of refugees. By 2002, the Bosnian population in the city had grown to around 40,000, and a similar number lived in Chicago. Some Bosnians moved to communities that were much smaller. In the town of Bowling Green, Kentucky, the Bosnian population had grown to 2,500 by 2001. Tatjana Sahanic, one of the newcomers, said: "The community was shocked by our arrival. They didn't know anything about us; we didn't know anything about them." Given time, though, most of them have found employment, and some have started businesses and purchased homes, becoming valued members of the community.

In 1995, a peace agreement officially ended the war in Bosnia and Herzegovina. A few years later, less than 10 percent of the people displaced by the fighting had been able to return home. Meanwhile, another crisis had arisen in Kosovo.

In February 1998, severe fighting broke out in Kosovo between Yugoslav Serbian forces and the Kosovo Liberation Army (KLA). The KLA was a military force established in 1997 to fight for the ethnic Albanians in Kosovo. Although the

United Nations and other organizations tried to negotiate an end to this war, the situation had worsened by the beginning of 1999. It became clear that Yugoslav president Slobodan Milosevic and his Serbian allies had little interest in a negotiated settlement. After peace talks collapsed in March, North Atlantic Treaty Organization (NATO) forces began attacking Yugoslav targets from the air in an attempt to prevent a Serbian takeover of Kosovo.

Serbian forces responded by moving into Kosovo and expelling as much of the Albanian population as possible. Mentor Nimani, a Kosovar Albanian human rights attorney, described the events after the Serb attack on Kosovo before the Senate Immigration Subcommittee on April 14, 1999:

> In Tirana [the capital of Albania], I began to talk to other refugees and document their stories. They spoke to me of the ordeals they had suffered and the atrocities they had witnessed. I spoke to one group of refugees from Peja [a city in Kosovo]. They told me that Serb authorities had expelled them from Kosovo and ordered them to walk to Albania. The men were separated from the women and they were threatened with death if they did not come up with money. To spare the men, the group gave the authorities all their money. On the way to Albania, two children and an elderly woman died. The group traveled without food or water. But, their worst experience was when they reached the border. There, Serb authorities forced them to stay the night. While they were trying to sleep in the open, loud speakers played. On the loud speakers they heard the voices of children screaming as if they were being killed. They also heard

A large segment of the refugees of the war in Bosnia and Herzegovina resettled in Chicago (above), St. Louis, and smaller communities of the Midwest. Many towns that had no Eastern European immigrants before suddenly had bustling Bosnian communities.

continuous threats of atrocities that would be committed against them, including descriptions of how they would be killed. One woman I spoke with said that this was the worst experience of her life. She will never be able to recover from this.

Another man and woman from Gakova [a town in northwest Serbia] described their escape from that city. Soldiers shot at them as they fled. They believe that eighty percent of the city has been set on fire and destroyed. In one mosque they passed in Gakova as they fled, they saw as many as 300 bodies of people slain.

The NATO air campaign lasted for 78 days. It was called a "humanitarian war" because it was meant to stop the fighting on the ground, but it also made the refugee crisis even worse. After the start of the air campaign, violence against the ethnic Albanians increased. In a short period, 800,000 ethnic Albanians had fled Kosovo. Many of them headed for the Macedonian border, to the south. Soon, Macedonian officials closed the border, stating that the country could not cope at that time with such a huge wave of refugees. But when it received pressure from UNHCR and NATO, Macedonia agreed to open its borders again, but it did so on the condition that other countries would help to evacuate the Albanian refugees. These "third countries" would accept the refugees for temporary or permanent resettlement.

About 95,000 refugees went to host countries around the world. Approximately 4,000 Kosovar Albanians were interviewed overseas and, to assure their protection, airlifted to Fort Dix in New Jersey to complete the interview process. Eventually, a total of more than 10,000 refuges entered the United States, while more than 7,000 went to Canada. The American program that brought the refugees directly to the United States was called "Operation Provide Refuge." The U.S. government loaned money to the refugees to cover travel costs to the United States; it was decided later that this loan did not have to be paid back.

In an unprecedented move for the U.S. refugee settlement program, the government also offered to pay for any refugee's return to Kosovo after the crisis ended. The deadline for registering in the funded return program was May 1, 2000. When that date arrived, one-third of the refugees had returned to Kosovo or had applied to return. Many others had decided to stay in the United States, or had not yet made up their minds.

In Canada, the refugees first went to military bases in Ontario and other eastern provinces. They were then resettled in towns and cities all over the country. For a period of two years, monthly payments from the government helped the

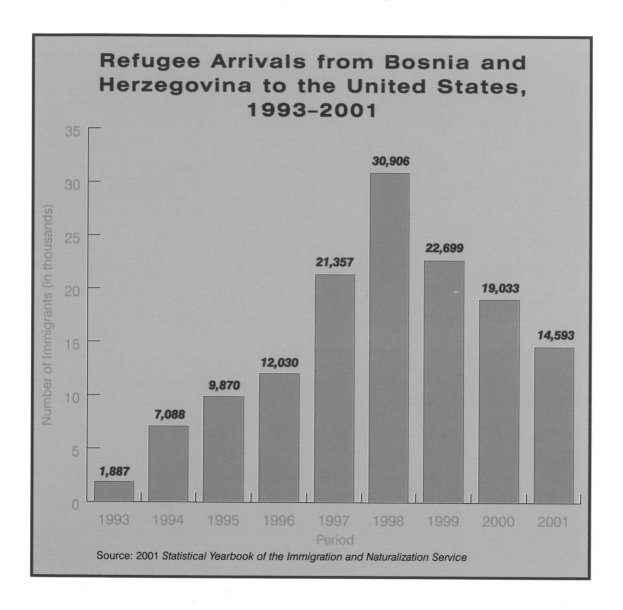

Refugee Arrivals from Bosnia and Herzegovina to the United States, 1993–2001

Source: 2001 *Statistical Yearbook of the Immigration and Naturalization Service*

A U.S. Army sergeant entertains children at the Mother and Child Refugee Center in Simin, Han, Bosnia and Herzegovina, January 1998. Some of the center's children, who lost their fathers in the Balkan conflicts, would later be accepted as refugees by the United States and Canada.

refugees get established. Sponsorship groups gave them practical help with shopping, registering their children in schools, and finding their way around their new communities. In some cases, Canadian individual and families took refugees into their own homes. One Canadian immigration official said of the people's attitude toward the refugees: "The next best thing to motherhood and apple pie was to have a Kosovar in your spare bedroom." By March 2000, only 1,900 of the more than 7,000 Kosovar refugees in Canada had chosen to return home. Although some were eager to go back to Kosovo as soon as possible, others decided that they wanted to stay in Canada permanently.

Many of the refugees felt that they had little to return to. They had lost their homes, their jobs, and even their friends and family members. But the welcoming attitude of most Canadians also encouraged them to stay. "I love Canada," said one refugee named Nita. "The people are very kind. I will stay here."

7 THE CHALLENGES AHEAD

The relationship between North America and those who arrive on its shores as refugees has never been without trials. Both refugees and the people who facilitate their arrival aim to continually make the admission process easier and fairer. The United States and Canada have worked hard toward reaching their goals for refugees, and at the start of the 21st century, both nations are recognized as world leaders in refugee assistance, though challenges remain.

In the United States and Canada, refugee assistance workers strive to maintain that position as international leaders. In addition to addressing particular refugee issues at home, organization leaders are often concerned with the bigger picture of how international policy affects refugees around the world. Organizations like the U.S. Refugee Committee and UNHCR address the conditions that cause refugee crises, such as poverty, civil war, and various forms of persecution. The prevention of future refugee crises rests largely on peace negotiations as well as the large-scale humanitarian efforts of organizations to redevelop destabilized countries.

International leaders are not the only ones able to improve the plight of refugees, however. There are things that every private citizen can do to help, such as donating to refugee aid organizations or volunteering for organizations like the United Nations Children's Fund (UNICEF) and the U.S. Association for UNHCR. Americans and Canadians with neighbors,

◀ Internally displaced Liberians wait to be distributed food outside the capital city of Monrovia, July 2003. Organizations like the U.S. Refugee Committee and UNHCR continue to offer assistance to the displaced people of the world, although their staggering numbers make such a goal very challenging.

The Challenge for the Children

In most refugee movements, at least half of the refugees are children under the age of 18. The situation of these young people is especially sad and difficult. It is hard for them to make their voices heard and protect their basic rights. Their lives become even harder if they are separated from their parents and families, or if their parents have died. Refugee children can often be resettled with relatives or host families in new countries. Unfortunately, others end up being detained or sent back to an uncertain future in their home country.

In 1993, UNHCR adopted the Policy on Refugee Children, put forward in a document entitled "The Challenge: The Special Needs of Refugee Children." It reads: "Children, including refugee children, are the future. They need special protection and care to realize their potential." The policy focuses on keeping families together, treating all refugee children equally, and protecting the children from the risks that they may face as refugees.

When they arrive in their host countries, many refugee children suffer from physical or psychological problems that have emerged after their experiences. In some parts of the United States and Canada, there are special programs to help refugee children to feel safe and happy in their new countries. In Toronto, Canada, a school program called Building Bridges helps refugee children to talk about their problems freely, to express themselves through art, and to make new friends.

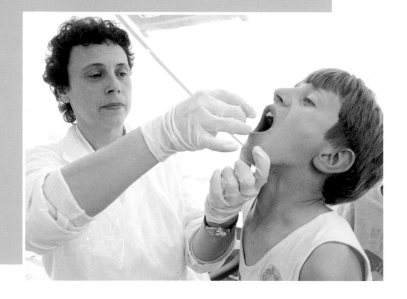

The Policy on Refugee Children, adopted by the UNHCR in 1993, was designed to address the physical needs of children like this young Albanian.

schoolmates, workmates, and friends who were or are refugees can have an even more direct impact.

Showing an interest in refugees and their unique history is a good way to offer support. Refugees face difficulties that many typical North Americans have not faced: they have been uprooted and thrust into a society in which things such as language, culture, food, money, and even weather can be completely new and different. Newcomers may appreciate it when someone takes the time to listen to their story, or suggests ways to help them adjust to their new life.

There is no reason to assume that refugees will immediately feel at home upon resettling. It may be true that many things are better for refugees in Canada or the United States than they were in their original home, but this does not mean they will immediately leave their former lives behind. Like all immigrants, refugees are encouraged to embrace new values and appreciate cultural differences. The level of comfort they feel as North American residents is affected by how their peers appreciate those differences in return.

That refugees even exist is one of the modern world's tragedies. Instead of reaching a resolution, this problem has continued and, in certain parts of the world, worsened. The U.S. and Canada, as well as some other countries, have taken up the challenge of helping those who have been forced to leave their homes. Everyone, from the most powerful government officials to schoolchildren, can help refugees as they adjust to the many changes and challenges that they face in their new homes.

FAMOUS REFUGEES

Valdas Adamkus (1926–), Lithuanian president and former senior official with the U.S. Environmental Protection Agency; he fled Soviet-occupied Lithuania for the United States in 1949, where he worked for the rights of Lithuanians and for the EPA, returned to Lithuania in 1997, and was elected the country's president in 1998.

Madeleine Albright (1937–), U.S. ambassador to the UN and first female Secretary of State (1996–2001); in 1939 she fled to England from home in Czechoslovakia to evade Nazi regime. She returned to Czechoslovakia, but after the Soviet regime came to power she fled again in 1948, this time to the United States.

Adrienne Clarkson (1939–), first foreign-born governor-general of Canada (the Queen of England's representative); she was born in Hong Kong, from which she fled when Japan invaded during World War II.

Albert Einstein (1879–1955), physicist responsible for some of the most important scientific discoveries in history; a public opponent of the Nazi regime, he left Germany in 1933 to avoid persecution.

Gloria Estefan (1958–), popular Cuban American singer whose albums include *Primitive* (1986, with Miami Sound Machine) and *Destiny* (1996); she arrived in the United States with her family, who had escaped Cuba to avoid persecution by Fidel Castro's regime.

Andrew Grove (1936–), founder and former CEO of the California-based Intel Corporation, one of the world's leading makers of semiconductors. He came to the United States as a refugee of the 1956 Hungarian Revolution.

Thomas Mann (1875–1955), Nobel Prize–winning novelist, author of *Buddenbrooks* (1901) and *The Magic Mountain* (1924); in 1936 he fled his home in Switzerland to avoid the threat of advancing Nazi forces.

Sitting Bull (1830–90), also named Tatanka Iyotake, Native American chief and leader of the Sioux tribe; he fought to protect his tribe when U.S. forces tried to take over its lands, and became a refugee when he led the Sioux to Canada, where the tribe remained for four years.

Elie Wiesel (1928–), survivor of the Holocaust born in Sighet, Transylvania. He became one of the world's most famous writers for *Night* and other books on the Holocaust, and won the Nobel Prize for Peace in 1986.

GLOSSARY

asylee—a person in the United States who receives refugee status, meeting the legal definition of an individual who has a well-founded fear of persecution.

asylum—protection given by a country to people who have come as refugees from another country.

Congress—the legislative body of the U.S. government, made up of the House of Representatives and the Senate.

democracy—a system of government in which the people participate, usually through elections.

ethnic—referring to a group of people who share the same culture, race, or nationality.

guerrilla—a person or group of people in a small, unofficial army, usually fighting against a country's official army or government.

immigrant—a person who has come to live in a foreign country.

interdict—to stop, prevent, or forbid.

internally displaced person—a person who has been forced to move from one place to another within a country, because of persecution, war, or other factors.

microcosm—a small community representing the qualities of something much bigger.

non-refoulement—the principle that a government cannot force people to go back to a country or region where their lives or human rights will be endangered.

refugee—a person who has been forced to leave his or her country because of persecution, war, or other threats.

regime—a system of government that is typically oppressive.

repatriate—to send someone back to a country of origin.

resettle—to move to a different place.

FURTHER READING

Adelman, Howard, ed. *Refugee Policy: Canada and the United States*. North York, Ontario: York Lanes Press, 1991.

Ager, Alastair, ed. *Refugees: Perspectives on the Experience of Forced Migration*. New York: Cassell, 1999.

Cutts, Mark, ed. *The State of the World's Refugees, 2000: Fifty Years of Humanitarian Action.* UNHCR. New York: Oxford University Press, 2000.

Daniels, Roger. *Coming to America: A History of Immigration and Ethnicity in American Life.* New York: Perennial, 2002.

Isbister, John. *The Immigration Debate: Remaking America.* West Hartford, Conn.: Kumarian Press, 1996.

Lewin-Epstein, Noah et al., eds. *Russian Jews on Three Continents: Migration and Resettlement*. London: Frank Cass, 1997.

Loescher, Gil. *The UNHCR and World Politics: A Perilous Path.* Oxford, England: Oxford University Press, 2001.

Meltzer, Milton. *Bound for America: The Story of the European Immigrants*. New York: Benchmark Books (Marshall Cavendish), 2002.

Pipher, Mary. *The Middle of Everywhere: The World's Refugees Come to Our Town.* New York: Harcourt Books, 2002.

Robinson, W. Courtland. *Terms of Refuge: The Indochinese Exodus and the International Response.* New York: St Martin's Press, 1998.

INTERNET RESOURCES

http://www.bcis.gov

The website of the Bureau of Citizenship and Immigration Services explains the various functions of the organization and provides specific information on immigration policy.

http://www.cic.gc.ca

Citizenship and Immigration Canada. Provides statistics on refugees in Canada and information on the government's refugee and immigration programs.

http://www.hrw.org/refugees

Human Rights Watch. An up-to-date resource covering refugee issues and the Human Rights Watch's campaigns.

http://www.irb.gc.ca

Immigration and Refugee Board Canada. Offers descriptions of the IRB's work, as well as instructions on how to apply for refugee status in Canada.

http://www.refugees.org

U.S. Committee for Refugees. Covers refugee issues, especially as they relate to the United States, and reports on the most recent developments involving refugees.

http://www.unhcr.ch/cgi-bin/texis/vtx/home

United Nations High Commissioner for Refugees. The official site of the organization, it gives updates on recent developments worldwide and provides opportunities to give donations toward refugee causes.

http://www.worldrefugee.com

World Refugee. A website of the WorldNews Network and a source for finding the latest news on refugees.

INDEX

1951 Convention, 22–24, 25, 42, 48
1976 Immigration Act (Canada), 40, 48
1952 Immigration and Nationality Act, 31
1965 Immigration and Nationality Act, 31–32, *34*
1967 Protocol, 23–24, 42, 48

ABC v. Meese, 63
    See also asylum
Adamkus, Valdas, 102
African refugees, 23–24
Albanians, ethnic, 91–92, 93–95
    See also Balkan refugees
Albright, Madeleine, 102
Amine, Hoda, 85
Ansari, Sanam, 83
Aristide, Jean-Bertrand, 70, 72
    See also Haiti
Ashcroft, John, 74
asylum, 42, 45, 47, 48–49, 63
    See also refugees
Austria, 20
Ayuen, Monica Tito, 15–16

Balkan refugees, 91–97
Barnes, Walter, 58
Batista, Fulgencio, *61*, 62
boat people, *51*, 55–56
    See also Indochinese refugees
Bosnia and Herzegovina, *87*, 92–93, *94*, *96*, *97*
Bureau of Citizenship and Immigration Services (BCIS), 35, 45–46, 47
Bureau of Customs and Border Protection (BCBP), 35
Bureau of Immigration and Customs Enforcement (BICE), 35
Bureau of Population, Refugees, and Migration (PRM), 45–47
Bush, George W., *35*

Califano, Joseph, 42
Cambert, Alex, 74–75

Cambodia, 51, 55, 58, 59
    See also Indochinese refugees
Canada, 17, 20, 25, 32–33, 56, 63, 83
    African refugees, 23
    Balkan refugees, 96–97
    immigration history, 38–41
    Indochinese refugees, 58–59
    refugee acceptance rate, 27–28, 51, 54, 81, 93
    refugee policy, 41–42, 48–49, 88–89, 99–101
Caplan, Elinor, 48
Cartagena Declaration (1984), 24–25
Carter, Jimmy, 66
del Castillo, Siro, 66–67
Castro, Fidel, *61*, 62, 64–66, 74–75
    See also Cuba
Central America, 24–25, 63
Chinese Exclusion Act of 1882, 28
    See also ethnicity
civil war, 15–16, 17, *24*, 25, 63
Clarkson, Adrienne, 49, 102
Clinton, Bill, 71
communism, 31, 39, 52–53, 62, 69, 71, 87–88, *89*
Comprehensive Plan of Action for Indo-Chinese Refugees (CPA), 57
    See also Indochinese refugees
Convention Governing the Specific Aspects of Refugee Problems in Africa, 24
Convention Relating to the Status of Refugees. *See* Geneva Convention Relating to the Status of Refugees (1951)
Cuba, 61–62, 64–66, 69, 71
    See also Cuban refugees
Cuban Adjustment Act, 68–69
    See also Cuban refugees
Cuban refugees, 61–62, 64–67, 68–69, 71–75
Czechoslovakia, 48, 89–90
    See also Balkan refugees

Numbers in **bold italic** refer to captions.

INDEX

Department of Homeland Security, 34–35
Detroit, Mich., 83–85
Displaced Persons Act of 1948, 30–31,
    41–42
        See also refugees
Duvalier, Francois (Papa Doc), 67, **68**
        See also Haiti
Duvalier, Jean-Claude (Baby Doc), 67, **68**
        See also Haiti

Einstein, Albert, 102
Eisenhower, Dwight, 88
El Salvador, 24, 63
Ellis Island, **27**
Enhanced Border Security and Visa
    Entry Reform Act (2002), 34, **35**
Estefan, Gloria, 102
ethnicity, 16, 18, 20, 28, 38–39

Fermi, Laura, 30
Ford, Gerald, 53
"freedom flights," 62, 64
        See also Cuban refugees

Geneva Convention Relating to the
    Status of Refugees (1951), 22–24, 25,
    42, 48
        See also Protocol to the 1951
        Convention (1967)
Germany, 19–20
"Golden Exiles," 62
        See also Cuban refugees
Gorbachev, Mikhail, 90
        See also Soviet Union
Grant, Madison, 30
Grove, Andrew, 102
Guantánamo Bay, Cuba, 70–71, 72, 73
Guatemala, 25, 63
Gulf War (Second), 84

Haiti, 61, 67–68, 69–70
Haitian Refugee Immigration Fairness
    Act, 73
        See also Haitian refugees
Haitian refugees, 61, 67–68, 69–71, 72–75

High Commission for Refugees. *See* U.N.
    High Commission for Refugees
    (UNHCR)
Homeland Security Act of 2002, 34–35
Honduras, 63
Hungarian refugees, 39, 48, 87–89
Hungarian Revolution (1956), 39, 87–88

Illegal Immigration Reform and
    Immigrant Responsibility Act (1996),
    33–34, 63
immigration
    history of, in Canada, 38–41
    history of, in the United States, 28–38
    rates of, in the United States, 30–31, 37
Immigration Act of 1924, 30
Immigration Act of 1990, 33
Immigration Act of 1952 (Canada), 40
Immigration and Nationality Act (1952),
    31
Immigration and Nationality Act of 1965,
    31–32, **34**
Immigration and Naturalization Service
    (INS), 32, 34, **46**
        See also Department of Homeland
        Security
Immigration and Refugee Protection Act
    (Canada), 40–41
Immigration Reform and Control Act
    (1986), 33
Indochinese refugees, 51–59
internally displaced persons (IDPs), 19,
    22
        See also refugees
International Refugee Organization (IRO),
    20–22
Iran, 77, 78–81
Iranian hostage crisis, 82, 83
Iranian refugees, 78–83
Iraq, 84, 85
Islamic Revolution, **77**, 78–80
        See also Iranian refugees
Israel, 84–85, 90–91
        See also Middle Eastern refugees
Italy, 20

INDEX

Johnson, Lyndon, *34*

Khamenei, Ali, 80–81
   See also Iran
Khomeini, Ayatollah Ruhollah, *77*, 78–80
   See also Iran
Kosovo, *87*, 91–92, 93–96

Laos, 51, 55, 58, 59
   See also Indochinese refugees
Laughlin, Harry N., 30
League of Nations, 16, 19, 21
   See also United Nations
Liberia, *99*
"Lost Boys," 16–17
   See also Sudan
Lynch, Jessica, 84

Mann, Thomas, 102
Mariel boatlift, 65–67
   See also Cuban refugees
McCarran-Walter Act (1952), 42
   See also refugees
Meissner, Doris, 47
"melting pot," 37
Middle Eastern refugees, 77, 83–85
Migration and Refugee Assistance Act
   (1962), 62
Milosevic, Slobodan, 92, 94
Mossadegh, Mohammed, 78

Nansen, Fridtjof, 16, 19
   See also U.N. High Commission for
   Refugees (UNHCR)
Nansen Medal, 27
Nicaragua, 24, 63
Nicaraguan and Central American Relief
   Act, 63
Nimani, Mentor, 94–95
Nine-Point Program, 62
Nixon, Richard, 88
non-refoulement, 22

Office of Refugee Resettlement, 45
Omidyar, Pierre, 82

   See also Iranian refugees
Operation Baby Lift, 53
Operation New Life, 53–54
   See also Indochinese refugees
Operation Provide Refuge, 95
   See also Balkan refugees
Orderly Departure Program (ODP), 56, *57*
   See also Indochinese refugees

Palestine, *20*, 84
   See also Israel
Panama, 25
Pearson, Lester, *39*, 40
Pickersgill, J. W., 88–89
points system, 40–41
   See also Canada
Policy on Refugee Children, 100
   See also U.N. High Commission for
   Refugees (UNHCR)
"Prague Spring" revolution, 89–90
Protocol to the 1951 Convention (1967),
   23–24, 42, 48
Puritans, 32–33

quotas, 28, *29*, 30, 31, 40

Refugee Act of 1980, 32–33, 42
Refugee Crisis of 1994, 71–72
   See also Cuban refugees
Refugee-Escapee Act (1957), 42
Refugee Relief Act (1953), 42
Refugee Status Advisory Committee
   (RSAC), 48
    See also Canada
refugees
   African, 23–24
   Balkan, 91–97
   Cuban, 61–62, 64–67, 68–69, 71–75
   definition, 17, 22–23, 45
   Haitian, 61, 67–68, 69–71, 72–75
   history of, 17–25
   Hungarian, 87–89
   Indochinese, 51–59
   Iranian, 78–83
   Middle Eastern, 77, 83–85

INDEX

policy regarding (Canada), 41–42, 48–49, 88–89, 99–101
policy regarding (United States), 41–47, 48, 68, 73, 95–96, 99–101
processing of, 46–47, 49, 70–71
rate of acceptance (Canada), 27–28, 51, 54, 81, 93
rate of acceptance (United States), *21*, 27–28, 43, *44*, 51, 56, *79*, 81–82, 93, *96*
al-Rehaief, Mohammed, 84
religion, 77, 80, 85, 90–91
resettlement programs, 42–43, 56–57, 88, 95–96
   See also Refugee Act of 1980
Ridge, Tom, 84
Right of Landing Fee (ROLF), 48
   See also Canada
Rosenblatt, Lionel, 55
Russia, 18–19, 90–91
   See also Soviet Union

Safe Third Country Agreement, 48–49
Sahanic, Tatjana, 93
Scully, C. D., 29
Sitting Bull, 102
slavery, 33
Socialist Federal Republic of Yugoslavia.
   See Yugoslavia
Soviet Union, 18–19, 71, 87–88, 90–91
   See also communism; Russia
Spain, 20
SS *St. Louis*, 41
Sudan, 15–17, 23, *24*
Temporary Quota Act of 1921, 30
   See also quotas
terrorism, 36, 43–44, 85

U.N. High Commission for Refugees (UNHCR), 16, 19, 22, 23, 25, 42, 46, 92, 95, 99–100
undocumented immigrants, 33–34, 35, 37, 75

United Nations, 20–23, 92
   See also League of Nations; U.N. High Commission for Refugees (UNHCR)
United Nations Children's Fund (UNICEF), 99
United States, 17, 20, 21, 25
  economy, 54, 66
  immigration history, 28–38
  immigration rates, 30–31, 37
  refugee acceptance rate, *21*, 27–28, 43, *44*, 51, 56, *79*, 81–82, 93, *96*
  refugee policy, 41–47, 48, 68, 73, 95–96, 99–101
U.S. Committee for Refugees, 15, 99
USA for UNHCR, 42
USA PATRIOT Act (2002), 34, *35*
USNS *Comfort*, 72
   See also Haitian refugees

Vietnam, 42, 51–52, 58, 59
Vietnam War (1957-75), 42, *43*, 51–55, *57*, 59
   See also Indochinese refugees
visas, 29, 32, 34, 36, 38

"wet foot, dry foot" policy, 73
   See also Cuban refugees
Wiesel, Elie, 102
World Refugee Survey 2000, 19, 24
World Refugee Survey 2002, 43
World War I, 17, 18, 29
World War II, *18*, 20–21, 22, 23, *29*, 30, 39, 41, 87

Yugoslavia, 92–94
   See also Balkan refugees

Zangwill, Israel, 37

CONTRIBUTORS

SENATOR EDWARD M. KENNEDY has represented Massachusetts in the United States Senate for more than 40 years. Kennedy serves on the Senate Judiciary Committee, where he is the senior Democrat on the Immigration Subcommittee. He currently is the ranking member on the Health, Education, Labor and Pensions Committee in the Senate, and also serves on the Armed Services Committee, where he is a member of the Senate Arms Control Observer Group. He is also a member of the Congressional Friends of Ireland and a trustee of the John F. Kennedy Center for the Performing Arts in Washington, D.C.

Throughout his career, Kennedy has fought for issues that benefit the citizens of Massachusetts and the nation, including the effort to bring quality health care to every American, education reform, raising the minimum wage, defending the rights of workers and their families, strengthening the civil rights laws, assisting individuals with disabilities, fighting for cleaner water and cleaner air, and protecting and strengthening Social Security and Medicare for senior citizens.

Kennedy is the youngest of nine children of Joseph P. and Rose Fitzgerald Kennedy, and is a graduate of Harvard University and the University of Virginia Law School. His home is in Hyannis Port, Massachusetts, where he lives with his wife, Victoria Reggie Kennedy, and children, Curran and Caroline. He also has three grown children, Kara, Edward Jr., and Patrick, and four grandchildren.

Senior consulting editor STUART ANDERSON served as Executive Associate Commissioner for Policy and Planning and Counselor to the Commissioner at the Immigration and Naturalization Service from August 2001 until January 2003. He spent four and a half years on Capitol Hill on the Senate Immigration Subcommittee, first for Senator Spencer Abraham and then as Staff Director of the subcommittee for Senator Sam Brownback. Prior to that, he was Director of Trade and Immigration Studies at the Cato Institute in Washington, D.C., where he produced reports on the history of immigrants in the military and the role of immigrants in high technology. He currently serves as Executive Director of the National Foundation for American Policy, a nonpartisan public policy research organization focused on trade, immigration, and international relations. He has an M.A. from Georgetown University and a B.A. in Political Science from Drew University. His articles have appeared in such publications as the *Wall Street Journal*, *New York Times*, and *Los Angeles Times*.

MARIAN L. SMITH served as the senior historian of the U.S. Immigration and Naturalization Service (INS) from 1988 to 2003, and is currently the immigration and naturalization historian within the Department of Homeland Security in Washington, D.C. She studies, publishes, and speaks on the history of the immigration agency and is active in the management of official 20th-century immigration records.

PETER HAMMERSCHMIDT is the First Secretary (Financial and Military Affairs) for the Permanent Mission of Canada to the United Nations. Before taking this position, he was a ministerial speechwriter and policy specialist for the Department of National

Defence in Ottawa. Prior to joining the public service, he served as the Publications Director for the Canadian Institute of Strategic Studies in Toronto. He has a B.A. (Honours) in Political Studies from Queen's University, and an MScEcon in Strategic Studies from the University of Wales, Aberystwyth. He currently lives in New York, where in his spare time he operates a freelance editing and writing service, Wordschmidt Communications.

Manuscript reviewer **ESTHER OLAVARRIA** serves as General Counsel to Senator Edward M. Kennedy, ranking Democrat on the U.S. Senate Judiciary Committee, Subcommittee on Immigration. She is Senator Kennedy's primary advisor on immigration, nationality, and refugee legislation and policies. Prior to her current job, she practiced immigration law in Miami, Florida, working at several nonprofit organizations. She cofounded the Florida Immigrant Advocacy Center and served as managing attorney, supervising the direct service work of the organization and assisting in the advocacy work. She also worked at Legal Services of Greater Miami, as the directing attorney of the American Immigration Lawyers Association Pro Bono Project, and at the Haitian Refugee Center, as a staff attorney. She clerked for a Florida state appellate court after graduating from the University of Florida Law School. She was born in Havana, Cuba, and raised in Florida.

Reviewer **JANICE V. KAGUYUTAN** is Senator Edward M. Kennedy's advisor on immigration, nationality, and refugee legislation and policies. Prior to working on Capitol Hill, Ms. Kaguyutan was a staff attorney at the NOW Legal Defense and Education Fund's Immigrant Women Program. Ms. Kaguyutan has written and trained extensively on the rights of immigrant victims of domestic violence, sexual assault, and human trafficking. Her previous work includes representing battered immigrant women in civil protection order, child support, divorce, and custody hearings, as well as representing immigrants before the Immigration and Naturalization Service on a variety of immigration matters.

CLARISSA AYKROYD is a graduate of the University of Victoria in British Columbia, Canada. She has written and published fiction, travel writing, and reviews of books, music, and plays. Her educational writing for children includes *Exploration of the California Coast*, *Native American Horsemanship*, *The Government of Mexico*, and *Egypt* for Mason Crest Publishers. She currently lives in Dublin, Ireland.

PICTURE CREDITS